A Practical Introduction to Computer Graphics

A Practical Introduction to Computer Graphics

Ian O. Angell

Department of Statistics and Computer Science,
Royal Holloway College,
University of London

A HALSTED PRESS BOOK

JOHN WILEY & SONS
New York

First published in Great Britain 1981 by
The Macmillan Press Ltd

Published in the U.S.A. by
Halsted Press, a Division of
John Wiley & Sons, Inc.,
New York

Reprinted 1982, 1983 (three times), 1984

Printed in Hong Kong

Library of Congress Cataloging in Publication Data

Angell, Ian O.
   A practical introduction to computer graphics.
   "A Halsted Press Book."
   1. Computer graphics. I. Title.
T385.A53   1981   001.64′43   81-11361
ISBN 0-470-27251-1   AACR2

Contents

Contents

Preface

Until recently, all but the most trivial computer graphics was the province of specialised research groups. Now with the introduction of reasonably priced graphics devices, the subject will reach many more users and its full potential can be realised. Computer-produced pictures always impress the layman, and the 'mysterious' techniques used for drawing them have gained a (false) reputation for complexity.

This book, as its title implies, is a practical first step in understanding the methods of computer graphics. After studying the contents and implementing the examples and exercises, the reader will be ready to attempt most tasks in graphics, whether these be the production of elementary data graphs, pie charts, etc., the drawing of patterns or diagrams for books, pamphlets or as teaching aids (all the diagrams in this book were drawn by computer) or the development of far more sophisticated design and technical drawing programs used in the aeronautics, automobile and other industries. Hints on how to tackle some of these sophisticated programs are also given.

It is assumed that the reader has an elementary knowledge of the Fortran IV programming language, and of cartesian coordinate geometry. This knowledge will be used to produce simple diagrams, and to produce the basic programming tools and routines required for the more 'complicated' designs. Then, hopefully, the reader will be inspired to seek a greater understanding of geometry and also to read more advanced works on computer graphics and to use the commercially available packages.

This book was designed to be completely self-contained, therefore no references are given. The contents reflect what I consider to be the logical development of the basic concepts in computer graphics, produced independently of the preconceived ideas of other authors, although standard terminology is used where appropriate.

The only way to understand any branch of computer science completely is to study and write a large number of programs; this is why the format of this book is that of 'understanding through worked examples'. The chapters are centred around numerous examples and the ideas that lead from them. Many students readily understand the theory behind graphics, but they have great difficulty in implementing the ideas. Hence great emphasis is placed on the program listings; over seventy program segments are given — some quite substantial. Total understanding will only be achieved by running these programs and experimenting with them. The programs can be thought of as an embryonic graphics package, but most importantly they are the means of describing the algorithms required in the solution of the given problems. They are readily translatable into other computer graphics languages such as Pascal or Basic. The routines described were devised for use with both Tektronix Interactive Graphics Consoles and microfilm, but again they can be made to run on any graphics system, be they paper plotters, other 'scopes, etc., with a minimum of thought.

The figures drawn are deliberately kept simple in order that the description of the detail in scenes should not obscure the new ideas being introduced. Complexity is left to the reader! No claims are made regarding the efficiency of the program segments; instead, a balance is maintained between efficiency of code and clarity of the description of the algorithm. As far as possible the programs were written in modular form. There are many cases where, by reorganising the programs, combining routines and perhaps obscuring the code, redundancy of data variables and statements may be eliminated. This can be considered a general exercise that runs throughout the book.

The main purpose of this book, which is essentially a third-year degree course given to undergraduates at Royal Holloway College, University of London, is to set out the groundwork of computer graphics, but to leave as much as possible to the imagination of the user — an exciting prospect. As one who found it 'difficult to draw a straight line with a ruler', I hope that my excitement in the discovery of computer graphics and its potential will become apparent in the following pages. I have been most gratified by the high standard and ingenuity of design produced by my students. In fact I have used diagrams produced by four of them: Hilary Green (figure 4.1), Jemma Coombe (figure 11.1), Helen Davies (figure 11.8) and Paul McLean-Thorne (figure 11.10). They have found that computer graphics is *fun*; I hope the reader will make the same discovery and spend many enjoyable and productive hours in front of a graphics console.

For those wishing to study computer graphics in more detail after reading this book, I recommend that they read W. M. Newman and R. F. Sproull, *Principles of Interactive Computer Graphics* (McGraw-Hill, 1973). It gives a good survey of the more complicated and theoretical aspects of the subject as well as containing an excellent bibliography.

IAN O. ANGELL

Acknowledgements

I wish to thank Professor H. J. Godwin for his help and encouragement and John Anderson for his valuable assistance with my computer graphics course. The photographic reproduction of all the diagrams and program listings in this book would not have been possible without the untiring work of J. G. Davies, to whom I am very grateful. Finally I would like to express my gratitude to my wife Florence for her cheerful support during the writing of this book.

1 An Informal Introduction to Two-dimensional Graphics

Before rushing into the more formal and mathematical aspects of the study of two-dimensional graphics it is a good idea for readers to familiarise themselves with those graphics devices to which they have access. A concise and formal grounding in the necessary mathematics is essential, but readers should first make a 'random walk' in the subject so that they may discover for themselves not only the potential of computer graphics but also that it is fun.

Any problem in computer graphics, whether it be two-, three- or multi-dimensional, reduces to specifying points in two-dimensional space and then marking individual points in some way, joining them in pairs with straight lines or filling in the areas bounded by such lines. The real problem lies in how to specify these points! This problem will be illustrated initially by a number of elementary examples, and in this way useful techniques and algorithms will be introduced before going on to the more formal approach in the chapters which follow.

All the programs in this book are given in Fortran IV, the computer language most widely used in commercial computer graphics. It is assumed that readers are reasonably competent in this language; in fact the following course in computer graphics will hopefully also raise the standard of their Fortran programming. The plotting routines used are all Calcomp-like, the necessary subprograms in the Calcomp library being described when the need arises.

There are obviously a large number of graphics devices commercially available, and these are of a variety of sizes; this book assumes the use of the standard Tektronix 4010 'scope, which has apparent plotting dimensions 22 inches horizontally and 16.75 inches vertically. (The true dimensions are approximately $7\frac{1}{2}$ by $5\frac{1}{2}$ in. but the software works in 'screen inches'.) The corners of the rectangular screen are initially defined to be $(-1.5, -1.0)$, $(20.5, -1.0)$, $(20.5, 15.75)$ and $(-1.5, 15.75)$, and so the coordinates of the centre of the screen are $(9.5, 7.375)$. (Note that all these numerical values are in 'screen inches'.) It is advisable for all readers to check the dimensions (real and apparent) of the devices they are using (X—Y paper plotters, microfilm plotters, 'scopes, etc.) and then to make the corresponding alterations to the example programs given in the following pages. See also project 17, p. 137.

We start by introducing just three routines from the Calcomp library.

(1)   START, the routine that prepares the screen for plotting, and defines the 'screen inch' and coordinate system;

(2)   ENPLOT, the routine that tidies up the screen after the plot is complete;

(3)   PLOT, the routine that moves the plot 'head' about the screen and actually draws the pictures; this obviously requires more discussion.

The use of the PLOT routine is always of the form

CALL PLOT(X, Y, N)

where (X, Y) is a vector pair (or coordinate pair) which gives the two-dimensional cartesian coordinates of a given point, and N may be called the movement information. (Here X and Y are REALs and N is an INTEGER with a value ±2 or ±3.) If N is ±3 then the plot head moves from its 'present position' to the point (X, Y) with the head up. The initial position of the plot head is the screen origin, and during the plot the present position is the last point accessed. If N is ±2 then the head is down during a move similar to that above, but in this case a straight line is drawn. When N is negative then a new coordinate system is initiated, with its origin at (X, Y) of the old coordinate system.

In order to explain these three routines it is essential that they be put into practice immediately. It is advisable for readers to implement a large number of the given examples (adding variations whenever and wherever possible), and attempt solutions to a large proportion of the exercises.

Example 1.1
Draw a square of side 8 inches, centred on the screen (a very simple program that is none the less very instructive).

```
      CALL START(2)
C CHANGE ORIGIN TO CENTRE OF SCREEN (9.5,7.375).
      CALL PLOT(9.5,7.375,-3)
C NOW SQUARE CORNERS ARE (4.0,4.0),(4.0,-4.0),(-4.0,4.0),(-4.0,-4.0)
C MOVE TO FIRST CORNER WITH HEAD UP
      CALL PLOT(4.0,4.0,3)
C NOW JOIN CORNERS WITH HEAD DOWN
      CALL PLOT(4.0,-4.0,2)
      CALL PLOT(-4.0,-4.0,2)
      CALL PLOT(-4.0,4.0,2)
      CALL PLOT(4.0,4.0,2)
C PLOT COMPLETE
      CALL ENPLOT
```

Program 1.1

Of course this is not the only way of drawing a square; in fact it is not even the most efficient way — the next section of code requires one less call to the PLOT routine.

```
        CALL START(2)
C CHANGE ORIGIN TO (5.5,3.375)
        CALL PLOT(5.5,3.375,-3)
C SQUARE NOW HAS CORNERS (0.0,0.0),(0.0,8.0),(8.0,8.0),(8.0,0.0)
C HEAD IS ALREADY AT (0.0,0.0)
C NOW JOIN UP CORNERS
        CALL PLOT(0.0,8.0,2)
        CALL PLOT(8.0,8.0,2)   *
        CALL PLOT(8.0,0.0,2)   *
        CALL PLOT(0.0,0.0,2)
C SQUARE COMPLETE
        CALL ENPLOT
```

Program 1.2

Note that in both these example programs the order in which points are joined is crucial — for example, if the two statements marked by an asterisk above are interchanged then instead of producing a square (figure 1.1a) the shape in figure 1.1b is drawn.

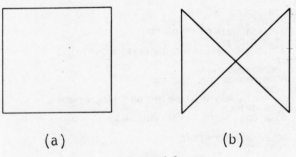

(a)   (b)

Figure 1.1

Exercise 1.1
Now draw a triangle, a pentagon and a hexagon with programs similar to those above. Also draw a picture that contains all of these figures on the same 'page' but with the polygons centred at different points.

The program in example 1.1 is such that all the points are explicitly given in the program. This is a relatively rare event; usually the points are implicitly calculated as the program progresses, as in the next example.

Example 1.2
Draw a circle, centred on the page, whose radius is a variable read by the program.

In Fortran all INPUT/OUTPUT is dealt with in channels; we assume that all INPUT uses the READ statement with channel 5 and OUTPUT uses the WRITE statement with channel 6.

Obviously it is impossible to draw a true curve with the currently defined PLOT statement: it only draws straight lines. However, we are rescued from this dilemma by the inadequacy of the human optical equipment — the failure of our eyes to resolve very small lines. If a continuous sequence of short lines is drawn, and this approximates to a curve then, provided the lines are small enough, our eyes convince our brain that a true curve has been drawn. This reduces the problem to one of specifying which lines are to be drawn. An arbitrary point on a circle of radius *r* and centre (0.0, 0.0) may be represented by the vector pair ($r \cos \theta$, $r \sin \theta$), where θ is the angle that the radius through the point makes with the 'positive *x*-axis'. Hence by incrementing θ in *n* equal steps between 0 and 2π radians, *n* points are produced, and these, if joined as they are calculated, define an equilateral polygon with *n* sides (an *n*-gon). If *n* is large enough then the *n*-gon approximates to a circle. The following program (which incidently is almost a solution to the first part of exercise 1.1) draws a circle (a 100-gon) of radius R, centred on the page.

```
      READ(5,*) R
      CALL START(2)
C MOVE ORIGIN TO CENTRE OF PAGE
      CALL PLOT(9.5,7.375,-3)
C MOVE HEAD TO FIRST POINT OF 100-GON
      CALL PLOT(R,0.0,3)
C SET THETA TO 0.0 AND CALCULATE INCREMENT 2*PI/100
      THETA=0.0
      THINC=0.062831853
C MOVE THROUGH POINTS OF THE 100-GON
      DO 1 I=1,100
C CALCULATE NEW THETA AND PLOT POINT ON CIRCUMFERENCE
      THETA=THETA+THINC
      CALL PLOT(R*COS(THETA),R*SIN(THETA),2)
    1 CONTINUE
C 100-GON (CIRCLE) NOW COMPLETE
      CALL ENPLOT
      STOP
      END
```

Program 1.3

The plot produced by this program is shown in figure 1.2a and, as previously stated, the 100 points are not stored but calculated as the program progresses. This program may also be used to demonstrate that it is essential to give all angles in a Fortran program in radians and *not* in degrees. In fact if the angles were in degrees — that is, THINC = 3.6 (360/100) — then the disastrous figure 1.2b is produced.

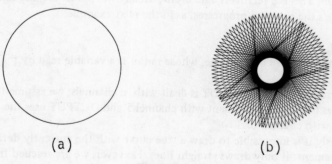

(a)   (b)

Figure 1.2

Exercise 1.2

Now draw an ellipse with a major axis of 6 inches and a minor axis of 4 inches (screen inches, of course!), centred on the page.

Note that a typical point on this ellipse may be represented as the vector pair $(6 \cos \theta, 4 \sin \theta)$, where $0 \leqslant \theta \leqslant 2\pi$; however, it must be remembered that this angle is not the angle made by the radius through the point with the positive x-axis; it is simply a descriptive parameter.

Exercise 1.3

Draw a diagram similar to figure 1.3. Note the optical illusion of two diagonal 'white' lines.

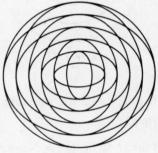

Figure 1.3

Example 1.3

Draw a spiral with six turns, which has outer radius 6 inches.

Note that a typical point on a spiral of n turns is again of the form $(r \cos \theta, r \sin \theta)$, where now $0 \leqslant \theta \leqslant 2n\pi$ and the radius depends on θ; in example 1.3, $r = \theta/2\pi$. Since there are many occasions when we need to draw a spiral about the coordinate origin, a general subroutine is given which will produce a spiral of N turns, outer radius R, whose initial direction is not along the positive x-axis but makes an angle ANG with it.

```
      SUBROUTINE SPIRAL (N,R,ANG)
C ROUTINE TO DRAW A SPIRAL OF N TURNS , OUTER RADIUS IS R UNITS
C ANG IS THE INITIAL DIRECTION OF THE SPIRAL WITH THE X-AXIS
      THETA=ANG
C INCREMENT=2*PI/100
      THINC=0.062831853
C MOVE TO CENTRE
      CALL PLOT(0.0,0.0,3)
C NN=TOTAL NUMBER OF POINTS CALCULATED
      NN=N*100
C RAD IS THE RADIUS INCREMENT
      RAD=R/FLOAT(NN)
      DO 1 I=1,NN
      THETA=THETA+THINC
      RR=RAD*FLOAT(I)
      CALL PLOT(RR*COS(THETA),RR*SIN(THETA),2)
    1 CONTINUE
      RETURN
      END
```

Program 1.4

In order to complete this example, the following call to the subroutine must be made

    CALL SPIRAL(6, 6.0, 0.0)

whence figure 1.4 is drawn.

Figure 1.4

Exercise 1.4
Using subroutine SPIRAL, produce another subroutine

    TWIST(X, Y, R, THETA)

which will draw diagrams similar to figure 1.5. Now (X, Y) is the centre of the figure relative to the screen origin, R is the radius of the circle containing the four spirals and THETA is the initial angle of one of the spirals.

Figure 1.5

It is now time to consider some 'nicer' examples, that is, to see how, with only the relatively few ideas we have used so far, it is still possible to draw aesthetically pleasing patterns.

Example 1.4
Produce a general program that places N points (N ≤ 100), equally spaced on the circumference of a circle of radius 6 inches, and then joins each point to every other.

Figure 1.6

Figure 1.6 shows the pattern produced by program 1.5 with N = 30. The N points are required over and over again, and so it is sensible to calculate them once only, store them in an array and recall them when necessary. The points are

$$(X_i, Y_i) = (6 \cos (2\pi i/N), 6 \sin(2\pi i/N)) \quad i = 1, 2, \ldots, N$$

Also note that if $i \geq j$ then the ith point is not joined to the jth point at this stage, since the line will have been drawn in the opposite direction.

```
      DIMENSION X(100),Y(100)
      CALL START(2)
C CENTRE PLOT
      CALL PLOT(9.5,7.375,-3)
C READ IN N AND CALCULATE THE POINTS
      READ(5,*)N
      THINC=6.283185307/FLOAT(N)
      THETA=0.0
      DO 1 I=1,N
      THETA=THETA+THINC
      X(I)=6.0*COS(THETA)
      Y(I)=6.0*SIN(THETA)
    1 CONTINUE
C JOIN POINT I TO POINT J FOR ALL I.LT.J AND I.LT.N .
      NM1=N-1
      DO 3 I=1,NM1
      IP1=I+1
      DO 2 J=IP1,N
      CALL PLOT(X(I),Y(I),3)
      CALL PLOT(X(J),Y(J),2)
    2 CONTINUE
    3 CONTINUE
      CALL ENPLOT
      STOP
      END
```

Program 1.5

Exercise 1.5
Program 1.5 is not a very efficient way of drawing the pattern; the plot head goes to and fro across the page and yet half of the time no line is drawn, since the plot head is just returning to the start point of each line. Write a program that draws the same diagrams, but is far more efficient than program 1.5.

Exercise 1.6
Draw a diagram similar to figure 1.7.

Figure 1.7

    This diagram (another 'pin-and-cotton picture' — so called after the child's toy) is drawn by first reading in the values of R and N. The program then calculates the coordinates of 4N points $\{P(I) \mid I = 1, 2, \ldots, 4N\}$ around the edges of a square of side R. There is one point at each corner and the points are placed such that the distance between consecutive points is R/N. Then pairs of points are joined according to the following rule: P(I) is joined to P(J) for all I and J such that $J - I$ is a Fibonnacci number less than 4N, the subtraction being carried out modulo 4N. (Note that the sequence of Fibonnacci numbers is the set of positive integers 1, 2, 3, 5, 8, 13, 21, 34, . . . , where each element is the sum of the previous two numbers. Because the indices of Fortran arrays always start at 1, we define modulo n as referring to the residue classes $1, 2, \ldots, n$, and *not* the usual $0, 1, \ldots, n-1$.) For example, if N = 10 then the point P(32) would be joined to P(33), P(34), P(35), P(37), P(40), P(5), P(13) and P(26). The outer square must also be drawn and thus, for efficiency, there is no need to join points which lie on the same side of the square.

Example 1.5
Emulate a Spirograph ®, to produce patterns similar to the one given in figure 1.8.

Figure 1.8

A Spirograph consists of a cogged disc inside a cogged circle, which is placed on a blank piece of paper. Let the outer circle have integer radius A and the disc integer radius B. The disc is always in contact with the circle. There is a small hole in the disc at a distance D (also an integer) from the centre of the disc, through which is placed a sharp pencil point. The disc is rotated in an anti-clockwise manner, but it must always touch the outer circle; the cogs ensure that there is no slipping. The pencil point traces out a pattern, which is complete when the pencil returns to its original position.

We assume that, initially, the centres of the disc and circle and also the hole all lie on the positive x-axis, the centre of the circle being the origin. In order to emulate the movement of the Spirograph it is essential to specify a general point on the track of the pencil point. We let θ be the angle made with the positive x-axis by the line joining the origin to the point where the circle and disc touch. The point of contact is therefore $(A \cos \theta, A \sin \theta)$ and the centre of the disc is $((A - B) \cos \theta, (A - B) \sin \theta)$. If we let $-\phi$ be the angle that the line joining the hole to the centre of the disc makes with the x-direction (note this angle has the opposite orientation to θ, hence the minus sign), then the coordinates of the hole are

$$((A - B) \cos \theta + D \cos \phi, (A - B) \sin \theta - D \sin \phi)$$

The point of contact between the disc and circle will have moved through a distance $A\theta$ around the circle, and a distance $B\phi$ around the disc. Since there is no slipping these distances must be equal and hence we have the equation $\phi = (A/B)\theta$. The pencil returns to its original position when both θ and ϕ are integer multiples of 2π. When $\theta = 2n\pi$ then $\phi = n(A/B)2\pi$; hence the pencil point returns to its original position for the first time when nA/B becomes an integer for the first time, that is, when n is B divided by the highest common factor of B and A. The function ICF given below uses Euclid's Algorithm to calculate the h.c.f. of two positive integers.

```
      FUNCTION ICF(II,JJ)
C.....FUNCTION TO FIND THE H.C.F. OF TWO POSITIVE INTEGERS II AND JJ
C.....II IS INITIALLY GREATER THAN JJ
      I=II
      J=JJ
    1 M=MOD(I,J)
      IF(M.EQ.0) GO TO 2
      I=J
      J=M
      GO TO 1
    2 ICF=J
      RETURN
      END
```

Program 1.6

Program 1.6 is used in a subroutine SPIRO which calculates the value n, and then varies θ (THETA) between 0 and $2n\pi$ in steps of $\pi/100$; for each θ, the value of ϕ (PHI) is calculated and thence the general track is drawn. Obviously the number of possible drawings is severely limited if the values of A, B and D are in (screen) inches, after all the page is only 22 by 16.75 inches. Therefore one of the parameters of the routine is a scaling factor which will allow us to use relatively large integers.

```
      SUBROUTINE SPIRO(A,B,D,SCALE)
      INTEGER A,B,D
      RD=D*SCALE
      RAB=(A-B)*SCALE
      THETA=0.0
      THETAD=3.1415926535*0.02
      AOVERB=FLOAT(A)/FLOAT(B)
      N=B/ICF(A,B)
      NO=100*N
      CALL PLOT(RAB+RD,0.0,3)
      DO 1 I=1,NO
      THETA=THETA+THETAD
      PHI=THETA*AOVERB
      X=RAB*COS(THETA)+RD*COS(PHI)
      Y=RAB*SIN(THETA)-RD*SIN(PHI)
      CALL PLOT(X,Y,2)
    1 CONTINUE
      RETURN
      END
```

Program 1.7

Figure 1.8 is drawn by making the call

CALL SPIRO(12, 7, 5, 0.4)

Exercise 1.7

Use this subroutine in a program which draws a large number of patterns on each page; the centres of each individual pattern need not be coincident. Then extend the subroutine so that the initial alignment of the centres and the hole need not be along the positive x-axis.

2 An Introduction to Two-dimensional Geometry

Users of any branch of programming must be fully aware of the underlying mathematical theory of the subject, in order that they will be less likely to misuse the various available packages. Also, when they build up their own library of procedures they will be fully aware of the limitations of these programs.

We introduce a variety of mathematical techniques: many will not be of immediate value, but they will immerse readers in the whole concept and potential of coordinate geometry. This, in turn, will lead to an appreciation of the fact that there is always more than one way of solving any given problem; the best solution will of course depend on the nature and context of the problem itself.

As usual, we work with the $x-y$ rectangular cartesian coordinate system; the positive x-axis is horizontal and to the right of the coordinate origin, the positive y-axis is vertical and above the origin. Thence, a typical point in this system is represented by the coordinate pair (sometimes called a vector pair) (x, y); these two values are the perpendicular projections of the point on to the respective x and y-axes. The vector pair may also be given in vector notation $p \equiv (x, y)$. Note that $\equiv$ means 'equivalent to'.

Next we look at straight lines; of course a line may be represented in the familiar form

$$ay = bx + c$$

where b/a is the tangent of the angle that the line makes with the positive x-axis, and c/a (if finite) is the intercept of the line on the y-axis (see figure 2.1). If c/a is infinite then the line is parallel to the y-axis.

A second way of representing a line (which, as we shall see, is more useful in computer graphics) is arbitrarily to fix two different points on the line $p_1 \equiv (x_1, y_1)$ and $p_2 \equiv (x_2, y_2)$; then the general point $p \equiv (x, y)$ on the line is given by the vector combination

$$(1 - \mu)p_1 + \mu p_2$$

for some real μ, that is, by the vector pair $((1 - \mu)x_1 + \mu x_2, (1 - \mu)y_1 + \mu y_2)$.

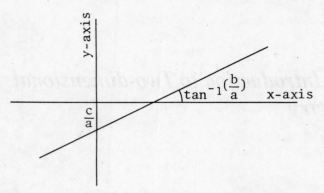

Figure 2.1

Furthermore, if $0 \leqslant \mu \leqslant 1$ then p lies on the line somewhere between p_1 and p_2. In fact μ is given by the ratio

$$\frac{\text{distance of } p \text{ from } p_1}{\text{distance of } p_2 \text{ from } p_1}$$

where the measure of distance is positive if p is on the same side of p_1 as p_2, and negative otherwise.

Example 2.1
Draw the pattern shown in figure 2.2a.

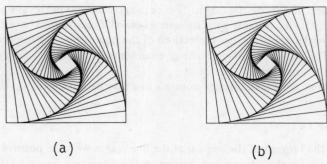

(a)   (b)

Figure 2.2

At first sight the figure looks quite sophisticated, but on closer inspection it is seen to be simply a square, outside a square, outside a square, etc. The squares are not only getting successively smaller; they are also rotating through a constant angle. Hence, to draw the diagram all we require is a technique which, when given a general square, draws a smaller internal square rotated through this fixed angle. Suppose the general square has four corners with coordinates $\{(x_i, y_i) \mid i = 1, 2, 3, 4\}$ and the ith side of the square is the line joining (x_i, y_i) to (x_{i+1}, y_{i+1})

(assuming additions of the indices are modulo 4, that is, $4 + 1 = 1$). Hence, a general point on this side (x'_i, y'_i) may be represented by

$$((1 - \mu)x_i + \mu x_{i+1}, (1 - \mu)y_i + \mu y_{i+1}) \quad 0 \leqslant \mu \leqslant 1$$

In fact $\mu:(1 - \mu)$ is the ratio in which the side is bisected. If μ is fixed and the four points $\{(x'_i, y'_i) \mid i = 1, 2, 3, 4\}$ of the new inner square are calculated in the above manner, then the sides of this new square make an angle $\alpha = \tan^{-1}[\mu/(1 - \mu)]$ with the corresponding side of the outer square. Thus, by keeping μ fixed for each new square, the angle between consecutive squares remains the constant α. In the program below (which produced figure 2.2a) there are 21 squares and $\mu = 0.1$, and thus the new corners are

$$(x'_i, y'_i) = \left(\frac{9x_i + x_{i+1}}{10}, \frac{9y_i + y_{i+1}}{10} \right)$$

```
      DIMENSION X(4),Y(4),XD(4),YD(4)
C INITIALISE FIRST SQUARE.
      DATA (X(I),I=1,4) /4.0,4.0,-4.0,-4.0/    /-4.0,0.0,4.0/  /-4.0,0.0,4.0/
      DATA (Y(I),I=1,4) /4.0,-4.0,-4.0,4.0/   /0.0,8.0,0.0/  /0.0,8.0,0.0/
      CALL START(2)
      CALL PLOT(9.5,7.375,-3)                  READ (1,*)SMU
C SET MU VALUE AND PRODUCE 20 SQUARES.
      SMU=0.1
      RMU=1.0-SMU
      DO 3 I=1,21
      CALL PLOT(X(4),Y(4),3)
C DRAW THE SQUARE AND CALCULATE THE COORDINATES OF THE NEXT SQUARE.
      DO 1 J=1,4
      CALL PLOT(X(J),Y(J),2)
      NJ=MOD(J,4)+1
      XD(J)=RMU*X(J)+SMU*X(NJ)
      YD(J)=RMU*Y(J)+SMU*Y(NJ)
    1 CONTINUE
C RESET SQUARE COORDINATES.
      DO 2 J=1,4
      X(J)=XD(J)
      Y(J)=YD(J)
    2 CONTINUE
    3 CONTINUE
      CALL ENPLOT
```

Program 2.1

There is an unsatisfactory feature of the pattern in figure 2.2a: the inside of the pattern is 'untidy', the sides of the innermost square being neither parallel to nor at $\pi/4$ radians to the corresponding side of the outermost square. This is corrected simply by changing the value of μ so as to facilitate the required relationship between the innermost and outermost squares. As was previously noted, with the calculation of each new inner square the corresponding sides are rotated through $\tan^{-1}[\mu/(1 - \mu)]$ radians. After $n + 1$ squares are drawn, the inner square is rotated by $n \tan^{-1}[\mu/(1 - \mu)]$ radians relative to the outer square. For a satisfactory diagram this angle must be an integer multiple of $\pi/4$ (t, say), that is, $n \tan^{-1}[\mu/(1-\mu)] = t(\pi/4)$, and hence

$$\mu = \frac{\tan[t(\pi/4n)]}{\tan[t(\pi/4n)] + 1}$$

To produce figure 2.2b, $n = 20$ and $t = 3$ are chosen, making $\mu \approx 0.08$.

Exercise 2.1

Repeat the previous example but, instead of using squares, use triangles, pentagons, hexagons, etc.

Exercise 2.2

Draw the pattern shown in figure 2.3. Produce a similar combination using triangles and hexagons.

Figure 2.3

Obviously the vector interpretation of lines is not necessary if a line is to be drawn between two points — we simply use

CALL PLOT(X1, Y1, 3)

CALL PLOT(X2, Y2, 2)

However, in later, more complicated uses, we shall want to consider variables on a line. Then this technique, or a variation of it, will be invaluable, and practice in its use (even just drawing patterns) will prove its worth.

Example 2.2

Draw a dashed line, with 13 dashes (and hence 12 equidistant spaces) between the points $p_1 \equiv (x_1, y_1)$ and $p_2 \equiv (x_2, y_2)$.

As we have seen, the general point on a line between these two points is $(1 - \mu)p_1 + \mu p_2$ for some μ; this may be rewritten in an equivalent form $p_1 + \mu(p_2 - p_1)$. In this new form, p_1 is called the base vector and $p_2 - p_1$ the directional vector; it is this new formulation that is used to solve example 2.2. The pen is moved to (x_1, y_1) with the head up. Then the vector $(1/25)(p_2 - p_1)$ is successively added to the initial point 25 times, each time moving the head to the newly calculated point. With each addition the 'mode' of the plot is alternated between 3 and 2, so that a dashed line is drawn. In fact $(1/25)(x_2 - x_1)$ and $(1/25)(y_2 - y_1)$ are stored, and these values are repeatedly added to the point (x_1, y_1) in the following subroutine, which draws a dashed line.

```
      SUBROUTINE DASH(X1,Y1,X2,Y2)
      CALL PLOT(X1,Y1,3)
C MOVE TO FIRST POINT WITH HEAD UP
C NOW CALCULATE X AND Y INCREMENTS
      XD=(X2-X1)*0.04
      YD=(Y2-Y1)*0.04
C MODE WILL ALTERNATE BETWEEN VALUES 2 AND 3
C ( I.E. HEAD DOWN OR HEAD UP )
C INITIALISE VALUES OF X Y AND MODE
      MODE=3
      X=X1
      Y=Y1
      DO 1 I=1,25
C CALCULATE NEW VALUES OF X Y AND MODE AND MOVE PLOT HEAD TO (X,Y)
      X=X+XD
      Y=Y+YD
      MODE=5-MODE
      CALL PLOT(X,Y,MODE)
    1 CONTINUE
      RETURN
      END
```

Program 2.2

Exercise 2.3
Draw a dashed line between two arbitrary points, so that the dashes are approximately 0.1 in. long and the spaces between them are about 0.05 in. long. Hint: the number of steps is no longer 25, but must be calculated by finding the distance between the two points, dividing this value by 0.05, then finding the nearest suitable integer to this value (it has to be of the form $3m + 2$ because the dashes are twice as long as the spaces between), and finally using this integer to calculate the true sizes of the dashes and spaces.

Example 2.3
Calculate the point of intersection $p \equiv (x, y)$ of the two lines joining:
(i) $p_1 \equiv (x_1, y_1)$ to $p_2 \equiv (x_2, y_2)$; and (ii) $p_3 \equiv (x_3, y_3)$ to $p_4 \equiv (x_4, y_4)$.

A general point on line (i) is $(1 - \mu)p_1 + \mu p_2$ for some μ, and a general point on line (ii) is $(1 - \lambda)p_3 + \lambda p_4$ for some λ. Thus the point of intersection p lies on both lines and all that is necessary to calculate p is to find the unique values of μ

and λ such that

$$p \equiv (1 - \mu)p_1 + \mu p_2 = (1 - \lambda)p_3 + \lambda p_4$$

that is

$$(1 - \mu)x_1 + \mu x_2 = (1 - \lambda)x_3 + \lambda x_4$$

and

$$(1 - \mu)y_1 + \mu y_2 = (1 - \lambda)y_3 + \lambda y_4$$

Hence

$$\mu(x_2 - x_1) + \lambda(x_3 - x_4) = (x_3 - x_1)$$

and

$$\mu(y_2 - y_1) + \lambda(y_3 - y_4) = (y_3 - y_1)$$

Thus, we have two equations in two unknowns, which are solvable if the equations are not linearly dependent, that is, if the lines are not parallel. Thus if

$$\Delta = (x_2 - x_1)(y_3 - y_4) - (x_3 - x_4)(y_2 - y_1) \neq 0$$

then

$$\mu = [(x_3 - x_1)(y_3 - y_4) - (x_3 - x_4)(y_3 - y_1)]/\Delta$$

and, having calculated μ, we can find p. For example, if $p_1 \equiv (-1, -2)$, $p_2 \equiv (1, 1)$, $p_3 \equiv (4, 5)$ and $p_4 \equiv (6, 7)$ then

$$\Delta = (1 + 1)(5 - 7) - (4 - 6)(1 + 2) = 2$$

and

$$\mu = [(4 + 1)(5 - 7) - (4 - 6)(5 + 2)]/\Delta = 4/2 = 2$$

and so

$$p \equiv (1 - 2)p_1 + 2p_2 = -1(-1, -2) + 2(1, 1) = (3, 4)$$

These ideas are incorporated in the following subroutine.

```
      SUBROUTINE INTER(X1,Y1,X2,Y2,X3,Y3,X4,Y4,X,Y)
C SUBROUTINE TO FIND (X,Y), THE INTERSECTION POINT OF THE TWO LINES
C FROM (X1,Y1) TO (X2,Y2) AND FROM (X3,Y3) TO (X4,Y4).
      DEL=(X1-X2)*(Y4-Y3)-(Y1-Y2)*(X4-X3)
C IF DEL IS ZERO THEN THE LINES ARE PARALLEL.
      IF(ABS(DEL).LT.0.00001) STOP
C CALCULATE "MU VALUE" OF (X,Y) ON FIRST LINE.
C THEN CALCULATE X AND Y.
      RMU=((Y4-Y3)*(X4-X2)-(X4-X3)*(Y4-Y2))/DEL
      X=RMU*X1+(1.0-RMU)*X2
      Y=RMU*Y1+(1.0-RMU)*Y2
      RETURN
      END
```

Program 2.3

Example 2.4

Find the angle that a line segment from the origin to the point $p \equiv (x, y)$ makes with the positive x-axis.

This problem, which is very common in all forms of graphics programming, introduces the trigonometric (SIN, COS, TAN) and inverse trigonometric functions (ASIN, ACOS, ATAN). SIN, COS and TAN are functions with one REAL parameter (an angle in radians) and a REAL result, SIN and COS in the range $[-1, +1]$, and TAN in the range $(-\infty, +\infty)$. The inverse functions have one REAL parameter in the above ranges and a REAL result in the so-called principal ranges: ATAN: $[-\pi/2, +\pi/2]$, ASIN: $[-\pi/2, +\pi/2]$; and ACOS: $[0, \pi]$. This leads us to the following subroutine, which is a solution to example 2.4; here, of course, the angle must lie in the range $[0, 2\pi)$. Note that $(a, b]$ means greater than a and less than or equal to b; $[a, b)$ means greater than or equal to a and less than b.

```
      SUBROUTINE ANGLE(X,Y,A)
C CALCULATE ANGLE THAT THE LINE FROM ORIGIN TO (X,Y) MAKES WITH X-AXIS.
      PI=3.1415926535
      PI2=PI*0.5
      IF (ABS(X) .GT.0.000001) GO TO 1
C LINE IS VERTICAL.
      A=PI2
      IF (Y.LT.0.0) A=A+PI
C IF LINE DEGENERATES TO A POINT RETURN ZERO ANGLE.
      IF (ABS(Y) .LT.0.000001) A=0.0
      RETURN
C LINE IS NOT VERTICAL SO TANGENT HAS FINITE VALUE.
C IF X.LT.0 THEN ANGLE IS NOT IN PRINCIPAL RANGE - ADD PI.
    1 A=ATAN(Y/X)
      IF (X.LT.0.0) A=A+PI
      RETURN
      END
```

Program 2.4

This routine will be used many times in the chapters dealing with three-dimensional objects.

Example 2.5

Calculate the acute angle θ between two lines, both of which pass through the origin.

This is where the concept of direction cosines of a line in two-dimensional space is introduced. These are the cosines (naturally!) of the angle that the line makes with the positive x and y-axes, respectively. If a line has direction cosines c_x and c_y — which can be considered as a directional vector $c \equiv (c_x, c_y)$ of the line — and passes through a point $p \equiv (x, y)$ (a base vector), then $p' \equiv p + \mu c$ represents a general point on the line. In fact p' is a distance $|\mu|$ along the line from p since $c_x^2 + c_y^2 = 1$; this is because, if the line makes an angle α with the positive x-axis, then $c_x = \cos \alpha$ and $c_y = \sin \alpha$, and we know that $\cos^2 \alpha + \sin^2 \alpha = 1$ for all values of α. Note that the symbol $|\ |$ represents the absolute value, that is, the size of the number ignoring the sign. If a line through the origin passes through the point (x_1, y_1), then the point $(x_1/\sqrt{(x_1^2 + y_1^2)}, y_1/\sqrt{(x_1^2 + y_1^2)})$ also lies on the line, and these new coordinates may be considered to be the direction cosines of the line. In general, if the line is $(1 - \mu)p_1 + \mu p_2$, which in the base/directional vector form is $p_1 + \mu(p_2 - p_1)$, then the direction cosines of this line are given by the vector $((x_2 - x_1)/r, (y_2 - y_1)/r)$ where $r = \sqrt{[(x_2 - x_1)^2 + (y_2 - y_1)^2]}$.

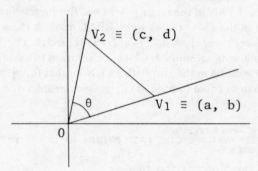

Figure 2.4

Returning to example 2.5, suppose that the two lines through the origin have direction cosines (a, b) and (c, d); see figure 2.4. Then $OV_1 = \sqrt{(a^2 + b^2)} = 1$ and $OV_2 = \sqrt{(c^2 + d^2)} = 1$, and by the cosine rule

$$V_1 V_2^2 = OV_1^2 + OV_2^2 - 2OV_1 OV_2 \cos\theta = 2(1 - \cos\theta)$$

But also

$$V_1 V_2^2 = (a - c)^2 + (b - d)^2 = (a^2 + b^2) + (c^2 + d^2) - 2(ac + bd)$$
$$= 2 - 2(ac + bd)$$

Thus $ac + bd = \cos\theta$. It is possible that $ac + bd$ is negative, and so $\theta = \cos^{-1}(ac + bd)$ is greater than $\pi/2$; the acute angle is then $\pi - \theta$ but, because $\cos(\pi - \theta) = -\cos\theta$, the acute angle is given immediately by $\cos^{-1}(|ac + bd|)$. For example, if the two lines have direction cosines $(\sqrt{3}/2, 1/2)$ and $(-1/2, -\sqrt{3}/2)$ then $ac + bd = -\sqrt{3}/2$ and thus $\theta = \cos^{-1}(|-\sqrt{3}/2|) = \cos^{-1}(|\sqrt{3}/2|) = \pi/6$. The FUNCTION that solves example 2.5 is as follows.

```
FUNCTION ANGLIN(A,B,C,D)
ANGLIN=ACOS(ABS(A*C+B*D)/SQRT((A*A+B*B)*(C*C+D*D)))
RETURN
END
```

Program 2.5

If the lines do not pass through the origin, that is, if they are of the general form $p_1 + \mu(a, b)$ and $p_2 + \lambda(c, d)$, then the acute angle between the lines is the same as the angle between the lines $\mu(a, b)$ and $\lambda(c, d)$, both of which have the origin as their base point; and we can use the above routine to calculate the angle.

DRAWING A GENERAL CURVE IN TWO-DIMENSIONAL SPACE

We have already shown how to draw certain well-behaved curves, such as circles, ellipses and spirals, in chapter 1: simply introduce a single variable and express the x and y-coordinates of a general point on the curve in terms of this variable. By allowing the variable to move through its complete range in small steps, a good approximation to the curve is produced. Thus, a circle of radius r is drawn by introducing the single variable θ, whence the general point on the curve is $(r \cos \theta, r \sin \theta)$, where θ varies between 0 and 2π. It may be possible that the variable is the x or y value itself, for example, when y is a simple function of x, as in the case $y = \sin x$. By varying x from -8.0 to 8.0 in steps of 0.01, the corresponding value of y ($\sin x$) is produced, and consecutive points are joined to give figure 2.5. The axes have also been added and labelled — see project 1, chapter 11.

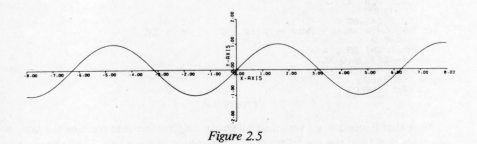

Figure 2.5

Exercise 2.4
Draw the curve $y = (\sin x)/x$; what happens at $x = 0$?

It is not always possible to use this simple technique, as in the case when the formulation of the curve is such that for each value of x there is more than one value of y, and vice versa. Take the simple coordinate form of a circle $x^2 + y^2 = r^2$. For each value of x there are two values of y, $\pm\sqrt{(r^2 - x^2)}$, and vice versa. To use this interpretation the value of x is varied from $+r$ to $-r$ in small steps, taking the y value to be the positive root $\sqrt{(r^2 - x^2)}$. When this sequence of points is joined, a semicircle is produced. The other semicircle is drawn by using the negative root as x returns from $-r$ to $+r$. The program using this method, which draws figure 2.6, is given below.

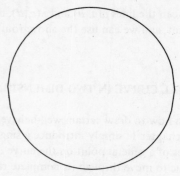

Figure 2.6

```
C F(X,Y)=36.0-X*X-Y*Y
      CALL START(2)
      X=6.0
      CALL PLOT(9.5,7.375,-3)
      CALL PLOT(6.0,0.0,3)
C GO THROUGH X VALUES FROM 6.0 TO -6.0   Y POSITIVE
      DO 1 I=1,60
      X=X-0.2
C ROUNDING ERRORS MAY CAUSE X*X TO BE GREATER THAN 36.0
      XS=AMIN1(36.0,X*X)
      Y=SQRT(36.0-XS)
      CALL PLOT(X,Y,2)
    1 CONTINUE
      DO 2 I=1,60
C GO THROUGH X VALUES FROM -6.0 TO 6.0   Y NEGATIVE
      X=X+0.2
      XS=AMIN1(36.0,X*X)
      Y=-SQRT(36.0-XS)
      CALL PLOT(X,Y,2)
    2 CONTINUE
      CALL ENPLOT
```

Program 2.6

Note that figure 2.6 is a very unsatisfactory diagram, because some of the line segments that form the 'circle' are noticeable as lines and not arcs. This is because, when x is almost equal to r, a small change in x makes a substantial change in y — so beware! This technique should therefore never be used to draw a circle on a high resolution graphics device.

Exercise 2.5
Use the above technique to draw the curve $\cos^3 y = \sin x$. Vary x from -8.0 to 8.0; note that there are an infinity of solutions of the above equations. Produce three curves, one from each of the ranges $[0, \pi]$, $[-\pi, 0]$ and $[\pi, 2\pi]$.

Since we are looking at functions in x and y, this is a good time to introduce the functional representation of curves. Suppose $f(x, y)$ stands for some combination of x and y, and perhaps some constants; then we say that the equation $f(x, y) = 0$ represents all the points (x, y) on a curve in two-dimensional space. For example, $f(x, y) \equiv r^2 - x^2 - y^2$ represents a circle of radius r. As we have seen, such a curve may be drawn by varying x over a range of values, calculating a value of y from the equation $f(x, y) = 0$. If the curve divides space into two parts then the functional representation tells whether a point (x, y) is on the curve or, if not, in which part it lies. The two parts of space are defined by the sign of the function $f(x, y)$. For example, the circle $f(x, y) \equiv r^2 - x^2 - y^2$ is such that if

(1) $f(x, y) = 0$ then (x, y) lies on the circumference of the circle;
(2) $f(x, y) > 0$ then (x, y) lies inside the circle;
(3) $f(x, y) < 0$ then (x, y) lies outside the circle.

Points (x_1, y_1) and (x_2, y_2) are on the same side of the curve if and only if the non-zero sign of $f(x_1, y_1)$ is equal to the sign of $f(x_2, y_2)$.

A straight line divides space in two, and thus its functional representation $f(x, y) \equiv ay - bx - c$ may also be used in a similar way. Thus if $f(x, y) > 0$ then (x, y) is on one side the line (call it the positive side), and if $f(x, y) < 0$ then (x, y) lies on the other (negative) side; naturally, if $f(x, y) = 0$ then (x, y) lies on the line. In the case of the straight line, $f(x, y)$ has another very useful property, namely, $| f(x, y) | / \sqrt{(a^2 + b^2)}$ is the perpendicular distance from (x, y) to the line; for example, figure 2.1 shows the case $f(x, y) \equiv 2y - x + 2$ and so the point $(0, 1)$ is a distance $| f(0, 1) | / \sqrt{5} = 4/\sqrt{5}$ from the line.

The property of dividing space in two, together with the simple means of deciding which side of a line is which, enables the definition of a very useful object, a convex body in two-dimensional space. This is any closed sequence of line segments such that a line joining any two points inside the body bounded by the line segments lies totally 'inside' the body. More formally, it is a set of lines formed by joining the points $\{ p_i \equiv (x_i, y_i) \mid i = 1, 2, \ldots, n \}$ in order, that is, the ith line joins p_i to p_{i+1}, where again the addition of subscripts is modulo n. We normally fix a point of reference inside the body (s, t) (say); then, by the convex property, each radius from (s, t) to any point inside the body will, if extended in both directions, cut the boundary of the body in two and only two points. The order of the points p_i is such that the angles made by the positive x-axis with the radii joining (s, t) to these points form a steadily increasing (or decreasing) sequence.

Thus the lines bounding the body may be represented by the functions

$$f_i(x, y) \equiv (x_{i+1} - x_i)(y - y_i) - (y_{i+1} - y_i)(x - x_i), \quad i = 1, 2, \ldots, n$$

This systematic definition was chosen because $f_i(s, t)$ has a constant sign for all $i = 1, 2, \ldots, n$, and thus the 'inside' of the body is defined to be all points (x, y) satisfying

$$\{(x, y) \mid \text{the sign of } f_i(x, y) = \text{the sign of } f_i(s, t) \text{ for all } i = 1, 2, \ldots, n \}$$

The boundary of the body is the set of points

$$\{(x, y) \mid \text{the sign of } f_i(x, y) = \text{the sign of } f_i(s, t) \text{ or } 0 \text{ for all } i;$$

also $f_i(x, y) = 0$ for at least one $i \}$

Hence the outside of the body is the set of points

$$\{(x, y) \mid \text{there exists at least one } i, 1 \leqslant i \leqslant n, \text{ such that}$$

$$0 \neq \text{the sign of } f_i(x, y) \neq \text{the sign of } f_i(s, t)\}$$

For example, consider the convex body defined by points $(2, 0), (0, -1), (-2, 0)$ and $(0, 3)$, with the origin $(0, 0)$ as internal reference point, shown in figure 2.7.

$$f_1(x, y) \equiv (0 - 2)(y - 0) - (-1 - 0)(x - 2) = -2y + x - 2$$
$$f_2(x, y) \equiv (-2 - 0)(y + 1) - (0 + 1)(x - 0) = -2y - x - 2$$
$$f_3(x, y) \equiv (0 + 2)(y - 0) - (3 - 0)(x + 2) = 2y - 3x - 6$$
$$f_4(x, y) \equiv (2 - 0)(y - 3) - (0 - 3)(x - 0) = 2y + 3x - 6$$

Note that $f_i(0, 0)$ is negative for $i = 1, 2, 3, 4$. Also $(1, 1)$ is inside the body because $f_1(1, 1) = -3, f_2(1, 1) = -5, f_3(1, 1) = -7$ and $f_4(1, 1) = -1$, which are all negative and thus of the same sign as $f_i(0, 0)$ for all i. The point $(1, -\frac{1}{2})$ is on the boundary because $f_1(1, -\frac{1}{2}) = 0, f_2(1, -\frac{1}{2}) = -2, f_3(1, -\frac{1}{2}) = -10$ and $f_4(1, -\frac{1}{2}) = -4$, whereas $(2, 1)$ is outside the body because $f_4(1, 2) = 2$ (positive).

This technique is required for project 2, chapter 11, but it is advisable to attempt the following exercise first.

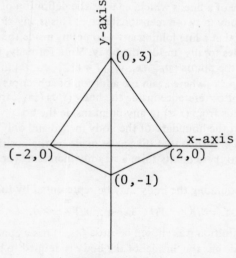

Figure 2.7

Exercise 2.6
Write a program that reads in information on a convex body and a reference point, and then reads in and prints out the coordinates of other points in space, together with a statement on whether these points lie inside, outside or on the boundary of the body.

3 Transformations of Two-dimensional Space; Matrix Representation

It is now time to consider what happens to an object, be it a point, line or curve, when the coordinate system is changed. As we have seen in previous chapters, all computer graphics reduces to specifying and joining points, and so all that is necessary is to discover what happens to the coordinate representation of points with a change of coordinate system. Up to now the coordinate origin, axes and dimensions defined for the two-dimensional space have been identified with the origin, axes and scale of the screen (the so-called observer coordinate system). This is not the general case, and so it is necessary to change from the old defined system to the observer coordinate system of the screen. There need only be three basic forms of coordinate-system change, that is, translation of origin, change of scale and rotation of axes; all other changes can be formulated in terms of these three types. Remember that initially the space is not changed; it is simply the position, direction and scale of the coordinate system used to define the position of points in space that are altered.

TRANSLATION OF ORIGIN

In this case, the coordinate axes of the old and new systems are in the same direction and are of the same scale; however, the new origin is a point (Tx, Ty) of the old system. Hence in the new system the old origin is $(-Tx, -Ty)$ and the general point (x, y) of the old system becomes $(x - Tx, y - Ty)$ in the new.

CHANGE OF SCALE

Now the origin and direction of axes are the same in both systems, but the scale of the axes is different; for example, 1 inch on the old x-axis could become 3 inches on the new x-axis, while the scale of the y-axis remains the same in both systems. Suppose a unit distance on the original x-axis becomes Sx on the new x-axis, and a unit distance on the old y-axis becomes Sy on the new. Then a point (x, y) in the old system has coordinates $(x \times Sx, y \times Sy)$ in the new; for example $(1, 1)$ becomes (Sx, Sy).

ROTATION OF AXES

The old system is shown in figure 3.1 with solid lines, and the new system with equi-spaced dashed lines; the systems have a common origin and scale. The new axes are the old ones rotated anticlockwise through an angle θ (the usual mathematical way of measuring angles). If the point P in the diagram has coordinates (x, y) in the old system and (x', y') in the new, then we have the relationships

$$x' = OX' = OB' + B'X' = AA' + P'P$$

$$= OA \sin \theta + AP \cos \theta = OB \cos \theta + OA \sin \theta$$

$$= x \cos \theta + y \sin \theta$$

$$y' = OY' = A'O - A'Y' = -AP' + AB'$$

$$= -AP \sin \theta + OA \cos \theta = -OB \sin \theta + OA \cos \theta$$

$$= -x \sin \theta + y \cos \theta$$

Any change of coordinate system between the originally defined system and the observer coordinate (screen) system will consist of a combination of these three types of transformation. However, it must be remembered that the order of their application is critical; transposing two such changes may result in a totally different system change to the one intended.

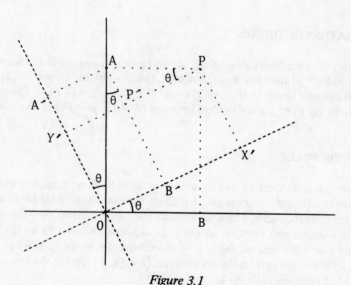

Figure 3.1

Example 3.1

Suppose the total change of system is achieved by

(1) move the origin to $(1, 0)$;
(2) rotate the axes through $\pi/4$ radians;
(3) change the x scale by a factor of 2 (that is, $Sx = 2$).

The combination of these three changes (in order) produces the observer coordinate system (the screen system). What happens to the line joining the point $(3, 2)$ to $(-1, -1)$ in the old system?

In all these changes, straight lines transform to straight lines, and so we need consider what happens to the coordinate representations of the vertices at the end of the line. After step 1

$$(3, 2) \xrightarrow{\text{becomes}} (2, 2) \quad \text{and} \quad (-1, -1) \longrightarrow (-2, -1)$$

After step 2

$$(2, 2) \longrightarrow (2 \cos \theta + 2 \sin \theta, -2 \sin \theta + 2 \cos \theta)$$
$$= (2/\sqrt{2} + 2/\sqrt{2}, -2/\sqrt{2} + 2/\sqrt{2})$$
$$= (2\sqrt{2}, 0)$$

and

$$(-2, -1) \longrightarrow (-2 \cos \theta - 1 \sin \theta, 2 \sin \theta - 1 \cos \theta)$$
$$= (-2/\sqrt{2} - 1/\sqrt{2}, 2/\sqrt{2} - 1/\sqrt{2})$$
$$= (-3/\sqrt{2}, 1/\sqrt{2})$$

After step 3

$$(2\sqrt{2}, 0) \longrightarrow (4\sqrt{2}, 0) \quad \text{and} \quad (-3/\sqrt{2}, 1/\sqrt{2}) \longrightarrow (-3\sqrt{2}, 1/\sqrt{2})$$

Thus on the screen the line is drawn as the line segment joining the two points $(4\sqrt{2}, 0)$ and $(-3\sqrt{2}, 1/\sqrt{2})$ of the screen coordinate system. To show that the order in which these transformations are carried out is critical, suppose we transpose steps 1 and 2. After step 2

$$(3, 2) \longrightarrow (5/\sqrt{2}, -1/\sqrt{2}) \quad \text{and} \quad (-1, -1) \longrightarrow (-\sqrt{2}, 0)$$

After step 1

$$(5/\sqrt{2}, -1/\sqrt{2}) \longrightarrow (5/\sqrt{2} - 1, -1/\sqrt{2}) \quad \text{and}$$
$$(-\sqrt{2}, 0) \longrightarrow (-\sqrt{2} - 1, 0)$$

After step 3

$$(5/\sqrt{2} - 1, -1/\sqrt{2}) \longrightarrow (5\sqrt{2} - 2, -1/\sqrt{2}) \quad \text{and}$$
$$(-\sqrt{2} - 1, 0) \longrightarrow (-2\sqrt{2} - 2, 0)$$

which are obviously different from the true screen coordinates above.

When large numbers of points have to be transformed then the transformations are stored as matrices using the following technique. The matrices used are 3 x 3 square, even though the space is only two-dimensional! This is because the translation of the origin requires a combination of x and y-values together with a linear distance which is independent of these values. Thus a point in two-dimensional space is represented by a column vector $\begin{pmatrix} x \\ y \\ 1 \end{pmatrix}$.

To translate the origin, the matrix operator must operate on this vector to produce a point in the new system of the form $\begin{pmatrix} x - Tx \\ y - Ty \\ 1 \end{pmatrix}$

This is achieved by the matrix

$$\begin{pmatrix} 1 & 0 & -Tx \\ 0 & 1 & -Ty \\ 0 & 0 & 1 \end{pmatrix} \text{ premultiplying } \begin{pmatrix} x \\ y \\ 1 \end{pmatrix}$$

Similarly the matrix for change of scale is

$$\begin{pmatrix} Sx & 0 & 0 \\ 0 & Sy & 0 \\ 0 & 0 & 1 \end{pmatrix}$$

and the matrix for rotation of axes is

$$\begin{pmatrix} \cos\theta & \sin\theta & 0 \\ -\sin\theta & \cos\theta & 0 \\ 0 & 0 & 1 \end{pmatrix}$$

Hence in example 3.1 we have the three matrices

$$\text{translation } T = \begin{pmatrix} 1 & 0 & -1 \\ 0 & 1 & 0 \\ 0 & 0 & 1 \end{pmatrix}$$

$$\text{rotation } R = \begin{pmatrix} 1/\sqrt{2} & 1/\sqrt{2} & 0 \\ -1/\sqrt{2} & 1/\sqrt{2} & 0 \\ 0 & 0 & 1 \end{pmatrix}$$

$$\text{scale } S = \begin{pmatrix} 2 & 0 & 0 \\ 0 & 1 & 0 \\ 0 & 0 & 1 \end{pmatrix}$$

By combining the matrices $S \times R \times T$ (x denotes matrix multiplication) we achieve the required change of system (note that the correct order of multiplication in the example is $S \times R \times T$ and *not* $T \times R \times S$ because the matrices *pre*multiply the column vector representing a point)

$$S \times R \times T = \begin{pmatrix} 2 & 0 & 0 \\ 0 & 1 & 0 \\ 0 & 0 & 1 \end{pmatrix} \times \begin{pmatrix} 1/\sqrt{2} & 1/\sqrt{2} & 0 \\ -1/\sqrt{2} & 1/\sqrt{2} & 0 \\ 0 & 0 & 1 \end{pmatrix} \times \begin{pmatrix} 1 & 0 & -1 \\ 0 & 1 & 0 \\ 0 & 0 & 1 \end{pmatrix}$$

$$= \begin{pmatrix} 2 & 0 & 0 \\ 0 & 1 & 0 \\ 0 & 0 & 1 \end{pmatrix} \times \begin{pmatrix} 1/\sqrt{2} & 1/\sqrt{2} & -1/\sqrt{2} \\ -1/\sqrt{2} & 1/\sqrt{2} & 1/\sqrt{2} \\ 0 & 0 & 1 \end{pmatrix}$$

$$= \begin{pmatrix} \sqrt{2} & \sqrt{2} & -\sqrt{2} \\ -1/\sqrt{2} & 1/\sqrt{2} & 1/\sqrt{2} \\ 0 & 0 & 1 \end{pmatrix}$$

Thus

$$\begin{pmatrix} 3 \\ 2 \\ 1 \end{pmatrix}$$

becomes

$$\begin{pmatrix} \sqrt{2} & \sqrt{2} & -\sqrt{2} \\ -1/\sqrt{2} & 1/\sqrt{2} & 1/\sqrt{2} \\ 0 & 0 & 1 \end{pmatrix} \times \begin{pmatrix} 3 \\ 2 \\ 1 \end{pmatrix} = \begin{pmatrix} 4\sqrt{2} \\ 0 \\ 1 \end{pmatrix}$$

and

$$\begin{pmatrix} -1 \\ -1 \\ 1 \end{pmatrix}$$

becomes

$$\begin{pmatrix} \sqrt{2} & \sqrt{2} & -\sqrt{2} \\ -1/\sqrt{2} & 1/\sqrt{2} & 1/\sqrt{2} \\ 0 & 0 & 1 \end{pmatrix} \times \begin{pmatrix} -1 \\ -1 \\ 1 \end{pmatrix} = \begin{pmatrix} -3\sqrt{2} \\ 1/\sqrt{2} \\ 1 \end{pmatrix}$$

which is consistent with the previous calculation.

These three types of matrices can be generated by the following three subroutines — TRAN2, SCALE2 and ROT2. In the programs Tx is TX, etc.

```
      SUBROUTINE TRAN2(TX,TY,A)
C CALCULATE 2-D AXES TRANSLATION MATRIX.
      DIMENSION A(3,3)
      DO 2 I=1,3
      DO 1 J=1,3
      A(I,J)=0.0
    1 CONTINUE
      A(I,I)=1.0
    2 CONTINUE
      A(1,3)=-TX
      A(2,3)=-TY
      RETURN
      END
```

Program 3.1

```
      SUBROUTINE SCALE2(SX,SY,A)
C CALCULATE 2-D AXES SCALING MATRIX.
      DIMENSION A(3,3)
      DO 2 I=1,3
      DO 1 J=1,3
      A(I,J)=0.0
    1 CONTINUE
    2 CONTINUE
      A(1,1)=SX
      A(2,2)=SY
      A(3,3)=1.0
      RETURN
      END
```

Program 3.2

```
      SUBROUTINE ROT2(THETA,A)
C CALCULATE 2-D AXES ROTATION MATRIX A.
      DIMENSION A(3,3)
      DO 1 I=1,2
      A(I,3)=0.0
      A(3,I)=0.0
    1 CONTINUE
      A(3,3)=1.0
      C=COS(THETA)
      S=SIN(THETA)
      A(1,1)=C
      A(2,2)=C
      A(1,2)=S
      A(2,1)=-S
      RETURN
      END
```

Program 3.3

Of course we need a routine for multiplying matrices in order to combine the
various transformations — subroutine MULT2.

```
      SUBROUTINE MULT2(A,B,C)
C 3X3 MATRIX PRODUCT.
      DIMENSION A(3,3),B(3,3),C(3,3)
      DO 3 I=1,3
      DO 2 J=1,3
      AB=0.0
      DO 1 K=1,3
      AB=AB+A(I,K)*B(K,J)
    1 CONTINUE
      C(I,J)=AB
    2 CONTINUE
    3 CONTINUE
      RETURN
      END
```

Program 3.4

Thus example 3.1 can be solved by computer with the following statements
calculating the required points.

```
      DIMENSION P(3,3),Q(3,3),R(3,3),S(3,3),T(3,3)
      CALL TRAN2(1.0,0.0,T)
      CALL ROT2(0.7853981643,R)
      CALL SCALE2(2.0,1.0,S)
      CALL MULT2(R,T,P)
      CALL MULT2(S,P,Q)
      X1= 3*Q(1,1) + 2*Q(1,2) + 1*Q(1,3)
      Y1= 3*Q(2,1) + 2*Q(2,2) + 1*Q(2,3)
      X2= - 1*Q(1,1) - 1*Q(1,2) + 1*Q(1,3)
      Y2= - 1*Q(2,1) - 1*Q(2,2) + 1*Q(2,3)
```

Program 3.5

Example 3.2

Draw an ellipse with centre (XC, YC), major axis A, minor axis B, in which the major axis makes an angle ϕ (PHI) with the positive *x*-axis (as in figure 3.2).

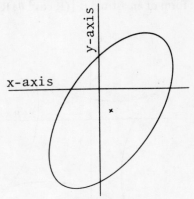

Figure 3.2

The functional representation of this ellipse is very involved and so the problem looks extremely complicated. However, by using the techniques defined in this chapter the problem is greatly simplified. Using the parametric form $\{(A \cos \theta, B \sin \theta) \mid 0 \leqslant \theta \leqslant 2\pi\}$ it is simple to draw an ellipse centred on the origin with major and minor axes coincident with the *x* and *y*-axes — the original coordinate system. By changing this system to the observer system using the procedure

(1)   rotate the axes through $-\phi$ (note minus, −PHI);

(2)   translate the origin to (−XC, −YC) (note minuses again),

the problem is solved — and the subroutine to draw such an ellipse is as follows.

```
      SUBROUTINE ELLIPS(XC,YC,A,B,PHI)
C ROUTINE TO DRAW AN ELLIPSE WITH MAJOR AXIS A AND MINOR AXIS B.
C CENTRED AT (XC,YC) WITH THE MAJOR AXIS MAKING AN ANGLE PHI WITH
C THE POSITIVE X-DIRECTION.
      DIMENSION P(3,3),Q(3,3),R(3,3)
C SETUP THE TOTAL TRANSFORMATION MATRIX R.
      CALL ROT2(-PHI,Q)
      CALL TRAN2(-XC,-YC,P)
      CALL MULT2(P,Q,R)
C TRANSFORM (A,0.0) BY R, AND MOVE TO THAT POINT ( PLOT HEAD UP ).
      X=A*R(1,1)+R(1,3)
      Y=A*R(2,1)+R(2,3)
      CALL PLOT(X,Y,3)
      THETA=0.0
      TDIF=0.031415926535
C FIND 200 POINTS ON THE ELLIPSE.  TRANSFORM THEM WITH R, AND JOIN
C THEM IN SEQUENCE.
      DO 1 I=1,200
      THETA=THETA+TDIF
      X1=A*COS(THETA)
      Y1=B*SIN(THETA)
      X=X1*R(1,1)+Y1*R(1,2)+R(1,3)
      Y=X1*R(2,1)+Y1*R(2,2)+R(2,3)
      CALL PLOT(X,Y,2)
    1 CONTINUE
      RETURN
      END                    Program 3.6
```

Exercise 3.1
Write a subroutine that draws an astroid (as in figure 3.3) of radius R, centred at (XC, YC), where one axis of the figure makes an angle PHI with the positive *x*-axis. The parametric form of an astroid is $\{(R \cos^3 \theta, R \sin^3 \theta) \mid 0 \leqslant \theta \leqslant 2\pi\}$.

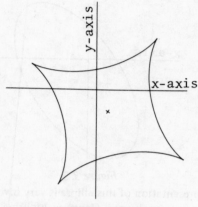

Figure 3.3

CHANGE OF SPACE

Instead of transforming the axes of a coordinate system we now consider what happens when the axes are fixed and the whole fabric of space is changed about them. Again there are three basic types of change.

Linear Transformation

The whole of space is moved by a vector (Tx, Ty); thus a point (x, y) relative to the axes is moved to a point $(x + Tx, y + Ty)$. This is exactly equivalent to keeping space fixed and changing the axes so that the origin of the old axes becomes $(-Tx, -Ty)$ in the new.

Stretching Space

The origin is fixed and the fabric of space is stretched by a factor Sx in the positive *x*-direction (and by the same amount in the opposite direction), and by a factor Sy in the *y*-directions. This is equivalent to keeping space fixed and scaling the *x*-axis by Sx and the *y*-axis by Sy.

Rotating Space about the Origin

If the whole of space is rotated by an angle θ about the origin, then it is equivalent to fixing space and rotating the axes through the same amount but in the opposite orientation, that is, by an angle $-\theta$.

This explains the minus signs and the order of transformations in the solution of example 3.2.

Exercise 3.2
Note that the translation and rotation of space do not distort figures; however, scaling may. Experiment with these transformations by considering polygons, spirals and other shapes already mentioned.

It is important to note that if matrices are read by statements like

READ(5, *)*A*

then the matrix is filled *by column* from the input channel, that is, the data input is understood to be in the order $A(1, 1), A(2, 1), A(3, 1), A(1, 2),$ $A(2, 2), \ldots,$ etc.

4 Clipping and Covering

We now have the ability to create graphical objects of arbitrary sizes and complexities in the observer coordinate system. Unfortunately the available graphical devices are of fixed sizes (usually rectangular). Thus, parts of an object that lie outside this boundary rectangle may cause problems. In most devices these external line segments are ignored; however, on some devices (in particular, microfilm plotters) these lines are reflected back into view causing (artistic!) confusion. This effect may be deliberately used to produce some unusual designs; figure 4.1 is such a diagram, which was drawn by one of my students.

Usually these lines will be suppressed. There are also times when we wish to draw only the lines lying inside a given rectangle, which is completely contained in the screen rectangle and thus of smaller size (and then perhaps expand the scale of the picture so that this new rectangle fills the screen). In both cases the

Figure 4.1

requirement is to *clip* off the line segments outside the specified rectangle. For example, clipping the line segments external to the outer rectangle in figure 4.2a will give figure 4.2b.

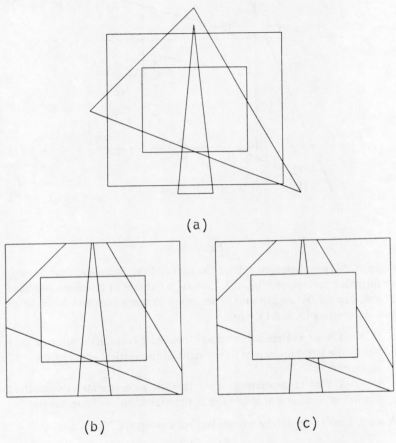

(a)

(b)   (c)

Figure 4.2

A SIMPLE METHOD FOR CLIPPING

The technique now described can be used to draw figure 4.2b, and also far more complicated diagrams such as figure 4.4. Initially, the problem is simplified by assuming that the coordinate origin is the centre of the rectangle, and the sides of the rectangle are horizontal and vertical, that is, if the rectangle is 2DX by 2DY screen inches then the vertices of the rectangle are (±DX, ±DY). Hence the problem reduces to that of discovering whether a line segment joining two points (x_1, y_1) and (x_2, y_2) has a subsegment inside the rectangle. The first step in the

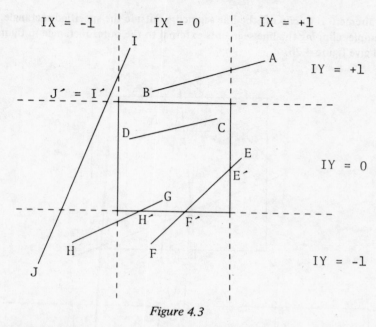

Figure 4.3

solution of this problem is to extend the edges of the rectangle, thus dividing space into nine sectors: see figure 4.3, where a number of line segments have been added to aid the explanation. Each point in space may now be classified by two parameters IX and IY where:

(1) IX = −1, 0 or +1 depending on whether the x-coordinate value of the point lies to the left, between or to the right of the vertical edges of the rectangle;

(2) IY = −1, 0 or +1 depending on whether the y-coordinate value of the point lies below, between or above the horizontal edges of the rectangle.

A subroutine to find these parameters for a point (X, Y) follows.

```
      SUBROUTINE MODE (X,Y,DX,DY,IX,IY)
C SUBROUTINE TO FIND FRAME MODE OF POINT (X,Y)
C DX*2 AND DY*2 IS THE SIZE OF THE FRAME CENTRED ON THE ORIGIN.
      IX=0
      IY=0
      IF (ABS (X) .GT.DX) IX=SIGN (1.0,X)
      IF (ABS (Y) .GT.DY) IY=SIGN (1.0,Y)
      RETURN
      END
```

Program 4.1

If the two points at the end of the line segment — that is, (x_1, y_1) and (x_2, y_2) — have parameters IX1, IY1, and IX2, IY2, respectively, then there are a number of possibilities to consider.

(1) If IX1 = IX2 ≠ 0 or IY1 = IY2 ≠ 0, then the whole line segment is outside the rectangle, and hence the line is totally ignored, for example, line AB in figure 4.3.

(2) If IX1 = IY1 = IX2 = IY2 = 0, then the line segment is totally inside the rectangle, and so the complete line must be drawn, for example, line CD.

(3) The remaining case has to be dealt with in detail. If IX1 ≠ 0 and/or IY1 ≠ 0 then the point (x_1, y_1) lies outside the rectangle, and a point (x'_1, y'_1) must be calculated. This is the point on the line segment nearer to (x_1, y_1) where the line cuts the rectangle. If it misses the rectangle, (x'_1, y'_1) is the point where the line cuts one of the horizontal edges extended. If IX1 = IY1 = 0 then $(x_1, y_1) = (x'_1, y'_1)$. A point (x'_2, y'_2) is calculated in a similar manner. See the algorithm described in program 4.2. The required clipped line segment is that joining (x'_1, y'_1) to (x'_2, y'_2). If the original line misses the rectangle then the algorithm ensures that $(x'_1, y'_1) = (x'_2, y'_2)$ and this new line segment degenerates into a point and is ignored. For example, EF is clipped to E'F', GH is clipped to GH' (G' = G) and IJ degenerates to a point I' = J'.

Thus the simplified problem is solved by the production of a subroutine CLIP such that, when given the two end points of the line segment (X1, Y1) and (X2, Y2) there are three possibilities: (1) exit the routine immediately; (2) a line is drawn between the two points; or (3) the clipped points (X1D, Y1D) and (X2D, Y2D) are produced and a line is drawn between them (if they are not coincident). The routine is then used on every line segment in the diagram to be clipped. Note that the dimensions of the clipping rectangle are stored in the COMMON block /OUTER/.

```
      SUBROUTINE CLIP(X1,Y1,X2,Y2)
C ROUTINE TO FIND CLIPPED POINTS (X1D,Y1D) (X2D,Y2D) CORRESPONDING TO
C POINTS (X1,Y1) (X2,Y2)
      COMMON/OUTER/DX,DY
C INITIALLY SET X1D,Y1D,X2D,Y2D TO X1,Y1,X2,Y2
      X1D=X1
      Y1D=Y1
      X2D=X2
      Y2D=Y2
C FIND FRAME MODES OF (X1D,Y1D) AND (X2D,Y2D)
      CALL MODE(X1D,Y1D,DX,DY,IX1,IY1)
      CALL MODE(X2D,Y2D,DX,DY,IX2,IY2)
C IF POINTS ARE IN THE SAME SECTOR OFF-SCREEN THEN RETURN
      IF(IX1*IX2.EQ.1.OR.IY1*IY2.EQ.1) RETURN
      IF(IX1.EQ.0) GO TO 1
C MOVE POINT 1 TO NEARER FRAME X-EDGE
      XX=DX*IX1
      Y1D=Y1D+(Y2D-Y1D)*(XX-X1D)/(X2D-X1D)
      X1D=XX
      CALL MODE(X1D,Y1D,DX,DY,IX1,IY1)
    1 IF(IY1.EQ.0)GO TO 2
C MOVE POINT 1 TO NEARER FRAME Y-EDGE
      YY=DY*IY1
      X1D=X1D+(X2D-X1D)*(YY-Y1D)/(Y2D-Y1D)
      Y1D=YY
    2 IF(IX2.EQ.0)GO TO 3
```

```
C MOVE POINT 2 TO NEARER FRAME X-EDGE
      XX=DX*IX2
      Y2D=Y1D+(Y2D-Y1D)*(XX-X1D)/(X2D-X1D)
      X2D=XX
      CALL MODE(X2D,Y2D,DX,DY,IX2,IY2)
    3 IF(IY2.EQ.0) GO TO 4
C MOVE POINT 2 TO NEARER FRAME Y-EDGE
      YY=DY*IY2
      X2D=X1D+(X2D-X1D)*(YY-Y1D)/(Y2D-Y1D)
      Y2D=YY
C NOW PLOT LINE BETWEEN THE NEW POINTS IF THEY ARE NOT COINCIDENT
    4 IF(ABS(X1D-X2D).LT.0.000001.AND.ABS(Y1D-Y2D).LT.0.000001) RETURN
C IF WE NOW WISH TO COVER (SEE LATER) PART OF THE FIGURE THEN
C THE FOLLOWING PLOT CALLS MUST BE REPLACED BY
C CALL COVER(X1D,Y1D,X2D,Y2D)
      CALL PLOT(X1D,Y1D,3)
      CALL PLOT(X2D,Y2D,2)
      RETURN
      END
```

Program 4.2

To solve the general problem, namely, when one pair of the rectangle sides make an angle α with the x-direction and the centre of the rectangle is (XC, YC), we use the techniques of the previous chapter. First calculate a matrix Q which translates the origin to (XC, YC), and a matrix P which rotates the axes through an angle α. Set $R = P \times Q$, and premultiply each point in the diagram by R. The problem now reduces to the simple case; however, each point has to be premultiplied by $R^{-1}(= Q^{-1} \times P^{-1})$ to return the points (including the clipped points) to their original coordinate form before the line segments are drawn; the problem is solved! Note that there is no need to calculate the inverse of the matrices P^{-1} and Q^{-1} directly, since P^{-1} represents the transformation of rotating the axes through $-\alpha$, and Q^{-1} is the matrix for the transformation of the origin to $(- XC, -YC)$.

Exercise 4.1
Clip figure 1.6 inside a diamond of side $6\sqrt{2}$. (The diamond is a square of side $6\sqrt{2}$ inches rotated through $\pi/4$ radians.)

A SIMPLE COVERING METHOD

Covering is the exact opposite of clipping. Again we have a rectangle (2DX by 2DY inches; DX and DY are now in the COMMON store labelled /INNER/), but in this case all line segments *inside* the rectangle are deleted. Figure 4.2c shows the result of covering figure 4.2b with the inner rectangle. This technique is normally used when information (such as messages) are to be written over a complicated diagram. Rather than cause confusion by overwriting part of the design, part of the diagram is blanked out by covering and the required message written inside the cover.

As with clipping, the problem is simplified by assuming that the cover has four corners $(\pm DX, \pm DY)$, and the transformations of chapter 3 can be used to manipulate the general case into this simple form, exactly as we saw with clipping.

Again space is divided into nine sectors by extending the edges of the cover. Each point in space is then given two parameters IX and IY using the routine MODE (program 4.1). Covering a line segment that joins the points (X1, Y1) to (X2, Y2) is achieved by

CALL COVER(X1, Y1, X2, Y2)

where the covering subroutine is as follows.

```
      SUBROUTINE COVER(X1,Y1,X2,Y2)
C ROUTINE TO FIND THE COVER POINTS (X1D,Y1D) AND (X2D,Y2D)
C CORRESPONDING TO (X1,Y1) AND (X2,Y2) RESPECTIVELY.
      COMMON/INNER/DX,DY
C CALCULATE THE MODES OF (X1,Y1) AND (X2,Y2)
      CALL MODE(X1,Y1,DX,DY,IX1,IY1)
      CALL MODE(X2,Y2,DX,DY,IX2,IY2)
      IF(IX1*IX2.NE.1.AND.IY1*IY2.NE.1) GO TO 1
C (X1,Y1) AND (X2,Y2) LIE OUTSIDE AND ON THE SAME SIDE AS ONE OF
C THE EXTENDED EDGES OF THE COVER, SO DRAW THE COMPLETE SEGMENT.
      CALL PLOT(X1,Y1,3)
      CALL PLOT(X2,Y2,2)
      RETURN
C CALCULATE POINT 1 , (X1D,Y1D).
C IF (X1,Y1) NOT BETWEEN THE X-EDGES MOVE POINT 1 TO NEARER X-EDGE
C ELSE (X1D,Y1D)=(X1,Y1) FOR THE MOMENT.
    1 IF(IX1.EQ.0) GO TO 2
      X1D=DX*IX1
      Y1D=Y1+(Y2-Y1)*(X1D-X1)/(X2-X1)
      CALL MODE(X1D,Y1D,DX,DY,IX1,IY1)
      GO TO 3
    2 X1D=X1
      Y1D=Y1
C IF (X1D,Y1D) NOT BETWEEN THE Y-EDGES MOVE POINT 1 TO NEARER Y-EDGE.
    3 IF(IY1.EQ.0) GO TO 4
      Y1D=DY*IY1
      X1D=X1+(X2-X1)*(Y1D-Y1)/(Y2-Y1)
C JOIN (X1,Y1) TO (X1D,Y1D) UNLESS (X1,Y1) ALMOST EQUAL TO (X1D,Y1D).
    4 IF(ABS(X1D-X1).LT.0.00001.AND.ABS(Y1D-Y1).LT.0.00001) GO TO 5
      CALL PLOT(X1D,Y1D,3)
      CALL PLOT(X1,Y1,2)
C REPEAT THE ABOVE PROCESS FOR POINT 2.
    5 IF(IX2.EQ.0) GO TO 6
      X2D=DX*IX2
      Y2D=Y1+(Y2-Y1)*(X2D-X1)/(X2-X1)
      CALL MODE(X2D,Y2D,DX,DY,IX2,IY2)
      GO TO 7
    6 X2D=X2
      Y2D=Y2
    7 IF(IY2.EQ.0) GO TO 8
      Y2D=DY*IY2
      X2D=X1+(X2-X1)*(Y2D-Y1)/(Y2-Y1)
    8 IF(ABS(X2-X2D).LT.0.00001.AND.ABS(Y2-Y2D).LT.0.00001) RETURN
      CALL PLOT(X2D,Y2D,3)
      CALL PLOT(X2,Y2,2)
      RETURN
      END
```

Program 4.3

The subprogram is explained with reference again to figure 4.3. If both of the points defining the line segment lie on the same side of one pair of rectangle edges (that is, IX1*IX2 = 1 or IY1*IY2 = 1) then the line lies completely outside the rectangle and must be drawn in total, for example, AB. When this is not the case we calculate (when necessary) the points (X1D, Y1D) corresponding to

(X1, Y1) and (X2D, Y2D) corresponding to (X2, Y2). If (X1, Y1) lies inside the rectangle, then (X1D, Y1D) = (X1, Y1); if it is outside, then (X1D, Y1D) is produced in the same way as in the clipping routine. (X2D, Y2D) is found in an equivalent way. The routine joins (X1, Y1) to (X1D, Y1D) if the points are not coincident, and similarly (X2, Y2) to (X2D, Y2D). For example, CD is not drawn because both C and D lie inside the rectangle; EE′ and FF′ are drawn, and since E′ = F′ these lines combine to give the complete line EF; GG′ and H′H are the two subsegments drawn from GH; and finally J′J is drawn from IJ.

Exercise 4.2
Draw figures 4.2a, b and c.

Exercise 4.3
Draw figure 4.4, which is figure 1.6 clipped by a square with side $6\sqrt{2}$ inches and covered by a square with side 2 inches. Both squares are centred at the origin — the centre of the circle of 30 points.

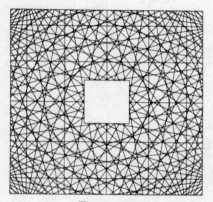

Figure 4.4

THE USE OF CURSORS AND PEN SENSORS

Many interactive graphics devices have cursors (moveable crosshairs) and/or pen sensors (for example, light pens), which enable the user to indicate individual points on the device screen or surface. By pressing a special button the keyboard (or other equivalent methods), the coordinates of the point specified by the cursor can be read by the program. A subroutine call, probably of the form

    CALL CURSOR(XC, YC)

will make the program pause until the key is depressed, when the coordinates of the point specified by the cursor are identified with the values of the variables XC and YC. Naturally the form of this type of input varies between implementations — so check!

Reading in a sequence of points in this way enables us to draw straight-line diagrams on to the screen, and perhaps store the input information in arrays. For example

```
CALL CURSOR(X(1),Y(1))
CALL PLOT(X(1),Y(1),3)
DO 1 I=2,4
CALL CURSOR(X(I),Y(I))
CALL PLOT(X(I),Y(I),2)
1 CONTINUE
CALL PLOT(X(1),Y(1),2)
```

Program 4.4

enables us to draw a quadrilateral, and to store the vertices in the arrays X and Y If the quadrilateral is meant to be a rectangle then the inaccuracies implicit in moving the cursor about the screen may lead to non-parallel lines in the rectangle. A simple way to correct this error is to use a *grid*. We imagine a grid of horizontal and vertical lines covering the screen, the origin being one of the points of intersection of these lines. The size of the grid (that is, GRID, the perpendicular distance between two neighbouring parallel lines) is left to the programmer, and its value depends on the accuracy required in the program. The coordinates of the points of intersection of the grid are not stored; they can be calculated whenever they are required. When a point is specified by a cursor, (XC, YC), instead of storing these values, we store the coordinates of the grid point nearest to (XC, YC); thus

```
CALL CURSOR(XC,YC)
X(I)=INT(XC/GRID)*GRID
Y(I)=INT(YC/GRID)*GRID
```

Program 4.5

where INT(R) is the Fortran function which returns the nearest integer to the REAL number R.

Exercise 4.4
Use the grid method to draw a number of polygons on the screen. Experiment by changing the GRID value.

If GRID is large then the number of grid points that the screen can accommodate is necessarily small, and so not many figures can be drawn. If GRID is small then the implicit errors in cursor movement may reappear.

Some computer configurations have a 'graphics pad' and either a pen sensor or digitising crosshairs linked into a graphics screen. Now the CURSOR call returns the coordinates of a point on the pad specified by the pen sensor. Thus coordinates of points on the pad can be stored in a data file and used to draw diagrams on the screen. In this way a rough sketch (of a mechanical component, for example) can be placed on the pad, scanned by the pen sensor and 'cleaned up' using the grid method to produce accurate drawings on the screen (and hard-copy on microfilm if required). Sophisticated packages based on this very elementary idea are proving to be of great value in the electronic and engineering industries.

A variation on this theme is the draw—drag—delete type of program. The idea is that the program contains a series of subroutines, each of which can draw an elementary figure (such as a diagrammatic picture of an electronic component) relative to a reference point. The program can *draw* any number of these figures on the screen (and in this way a complete electronic circuit can be designed). Each figure is placed by the cursor, which fixes the position of the figure's reference point. Again the grid method is essential to avoid distortions caused by non-horizontal and non-vertical lines implied by the cursor movement. Individual figures may be moved (*dragged*) about the screen, the change of position also being specified by the cursor. Finally it may be decided that a figure is unnecessary — it is pinpointed by the cursor and *deleted*.

MENUS

When the programmer has decided to draw, drag or delete, the required information has to be input. Of course it is always possible for the program to read the information from a keyboard; however, this tends to be tedious and error-prone, and so another method has been devised — the *menu*. A list of possible choices is drawn on the screen (or it may be a permanent fixture on a pad); each choice has its own box, which must be 'ticked' by moving the cursor (or pen sensor) into this area before the correct alteration can be made to the diagram. Naturally, all this writing will lead to confusion in the picture but, as we have seen, the ideal solution is to cover part of the screen and place the list of alterations with their boxes (the menu) inside the cover. The grid method should also be used to identify the unique box to be 'ticked'. (See project 3, chapter 11.)

This is a good time to describe how strings of characters may be written on the screen. Thankfully the programmer does not have to draw each individual character; all graphics packages have a subroutine that draws strings of characters. The one we describe (SYMBOL) is typical.

CALL SYMBOL(X, Y, HT, ICH, ANGLE, INDEX)

is the form of the subroutine call. There are a number of ways of using this routine; the uses are specified by the value of INDEX. We describe two uses: INDEX = −1 and INDEX > 0. In all cases (X, Y) are the coordinates of a point of reference used in drawing the string of characters, and HT is the height of the symbols. ANGLE is the angle (for some reason this is often given in degrees!) that the line of symbols make with the positive *x*-axis.

If INDEX = −1 then only one character is drawn; this is taken from a predefined list of symbols: ICH indicates which element in the list. The point of reference of the symbol will be either the centre of the symbol or its 'bottom left-hand corner' (check your manual).

IF INDEX > 0 then ICH will be the Hollerith string, of length INDEX, to be drawn on the screen.

In both cases each individual character is drawn in an imaginary square box. The following program will draw in the boxes around example output from SYMBOL in order to demonstrate how the routine works.

```
C EXAMPLES OF POSITIVE INDEX.
      CALL SYMBOL (-4.0,-4.0,2.0,3HXYZ,0.0,3)
      CALL SYMBOL (4.0,-4.0,2.0,3HXYZ,90.0,3)
      CALL SYMBOL (4.0,4.0,2.0,3HXYZ,180.0,3)
      CALL SYMBOL (-4.0,4.0,2.0,3HXYZ,270.0,3)
C EXAMPLES OF INDEX = -1.
      CALL SYMBOL (-1.0,-1.0,2.0,3,0.0,-1)
      CALL SYMBOL (1.0,-1.0,2.0,3,45.0,-1)
      CALL SYMBOL (1.0,1.0,2.0,3,60.0,-1)
      CALL SYMBOL (-1.0,1.0,2.0,3,85.0,-1)
```

Program 4.6

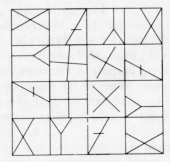

Figure 4.5

5 The Coordinate Geometry of Three-dimensional Space

It is now time to enter the real world of three dimensions. In order to introduce cartesian coordinates we necessarily require three mutually perpendicular axes, labelled x, y and z-axes, all of which meet at a common point, the coordinate origin. There are two independent ways of placing these axes, known as left-handed and right-handed triads of axes. In both types we may place the x and y-axes as in two-dimensional space, in the planc of the page (or screen) — the positive x axis placed to the right of the origin and the positive y-axis above the origin. This just leaves the placement of the z-axis (whence the two classifications of triads); it may be into the page (left-handed) or out of the page (right-handed). In this book we *always* use the left-handed notation.

We specify a general point p in space by the coordinate vector triple (x, y, z), where the individual coordinate values are the perpendicular projections of the point on to the respective x, y and z-axes. By projection we mean the unique point on the specified axis such that the line from that point to p is perpendicular to that axis.

A line in three-dimensional space passing through two such points $p_1 \equiv (x_1, y_1, z_1)$ and $p_2 \equiv (x_2, y_2, z_2)$ is the next type of object to be defined. This is accomplished by describing a general point $p \equiv (x, y, z)$ on the line by the three equations

$$(x - x_1)(y_2 - y_1) = (y - y_1)(x_2 - x_1)$$
$$(y - y_1)(z_2 - z_1) = (z - z_1)(y_2 - y_1)$$

and

$$(z - z_1)(x_2 - x_1) = (x - x_1)(z_2 - z_1)$$

These equations enable us to calculate two of the coordinates in terms of the third (see example 5.1).

As with two dimensions, this form is not the only way of representing a line in three-dimensional space; in fact the second way we introduce is possibly more useful. The general point on the line is now represented as a vector that is dependent only on one real number μ

$$p(\mu) \equiv (1 - \mu)p_1 + \mu p_2 \quad -\infty < \mu < \infty$$

that is

$$p(\mu) \equiv ((1 - \mu)x_1 + \mu x_2, (1 - \mu)y_1 + \mu y_2, (1 - \mu)z_1 + \mu z_2)$$

This form is equivalent to that described in chapter 2, and in fact the interpretation of μ is exactly analogous.

This form may be rewritten

$$p(\mu) \equiv p_1 + \mu(p_2 - p_1)$$

Here p_1 is known as the *base vector*, which, in fact, may be any point on the line, and $p_2 - p_1$ is called the *directional vector*. This is the first time we have come across the dual interpretation of a vector. We have used a vector as a means of uniquely determining a point in three-dimensional space; but it may also be considered as a general direction, namely any line parallel to the line joining the origin to the point vector (as interpreted above). Of course, we move along a line in one of two possible directions, and so we need to define the *sense* of a direction vector, namely that from the origin towards the point vector in space; the opposite sense is obviously from the point towards the origin. Now we can define the length (or modulus) of a vector p to be $|p|$, the distance of the point vector from the origin. Hence if $p \equiv (p_1, p_2, p_3)$ then

$$|p| = \sqrt{(p_1^2 + p_2^2 + p_3^2)}$$

Thus any point on a line $p + \mu d$ is found by moving to the base vector p and then travelling along the line through p, which is parallel to the direction vector d, a distance $\mu |d|$ in the sense of d if μ is positive, or a distance $-\mu |d|$ in the opposite sense to d if μ is negative. (Note that the sense of $-d$ is the opposite sense to that of d.)

The coordinates of a directional vector $d \equiv (d_1, d_2, d_3)$ tell us far more than just the modulus of the vector. For if $\theta_x, \theta_y, \theta_z$ are the angles that such a directional vector makes with the respective positive x, y and z-axes then the ratios

$$d_1 : d_2 : d_3 = \cos \theta_x : \cos \theta_y : \cos \theta_z$$

We know from the properties of three-dimensional geometry that

$$\cos^2 \theta_x + \cos^2 \theta_y + \cos^2 \theta_z = 1$$

Hence if the directional vector has modulus 1, then the coordinates of this vector must be $(\cos \theta_x, \cos \theta_y, \cos \theta_z)$; these coordinates are called the direction cosines of the set of lines generated by the directional vector. In general, if the direction vector is (d_1, d_2, d_3) then the direction cosines are

$$\frac{d_1}{|d|}, \frac{d_2}{|d|}, \frac{d_3}{|d|}$$

Example 5.1
Describe the line joining $(1, 2, 3)$ to $(-1, 0, 2)$.

The general point (x, y, z) on the line satisfies the equations

$$(x - 1)(0 - 2) = (y - 2)(-1 - 1), \qquad \text{that is, } -2x + 2y = 2 \tag{5.1}$$

$$(y - 2)(2 - 3) = (z - 3)(0 - 2), \qquad \text{that is, } -y + 2z = 4 \tag{5.2}$$

and

$$(z - 3)(-1 - 1) = (x - 1)(2 - 3), \qquad \text{that is, } -2z + x = -5 \tag{5.3}$$

Note that equation 5.1 is -2 times the sum of equations 5.2 and 5.3. Thus we need only consider these latter two equations, and we get

$$y = 2z - 4 \quad \text{and} \quad x = 2z - 5$$

whence the general point on the line depends on only one variable, in this case z, and it is given by $(2z - 5, 2z - 4, z)$. We can check this result by noting that when $z = 3$ we get $(1, 2, 3)$ and when $z = 2$ we get $(-1, 0, 2)$.

The line in vector form is

$$p(\mu) \equiv (1 - \mu)(1, 2, 3) + \mu(-1, 0, 2)$$
$$= (1 - 2\mu, 2 - 2\mu, 3 - \mu)$$

Again the coordinates depend on just the variable μ and, to check the validity of our line, we note that $p(0) \equiv (1, 2, 3)$ and $p(1) \equiv (-1, 0, 2)$.

Of course the line may be represented in the equivalent base vector and directional vector form

$$p(\mu) \equiv (1, 2, 3) + \mu(-2, -2, -1)$$

with $(1, 2, 3)$ as base vector and $(-2, -2, -1)$ the directional vector with modulus $\sqrt{(4 + 4 + 1)} = \sqrt{9} = 3$. As was previously stated, any point on the line can act as a base vector; hence

$$p'(\mu) \equiv (-1, 0, 2) + \mu(-2, -2, -1)$$

is another valid representation of the same line. We can change the directional vector into its direction cosine form $(-2/3, -2/3, -1/3)$ and represent the line

$$p''(\mu) \equiv (1, 2, 3) + \mu(-2/3, -2/3, -1/3)$$

Now, of course, the same value of μ will give different points on the line, for example

$$p(3) \equiv (-5, -4, -1), p'(3) \equiv (-7, -6, -1), p''(3) \equiv (-1, 0, 2)$$

The line through the origin with this directional vector makes angles $131.81° = \cos^{-1}(-2/3)$, $131.81°$ and $109.47° = \cos^{-1}(-1/3)$ with the x, y and z axes, respectively.

The next object to consider is naturally the plane. Before doing this we have to introduce the operator $\cdot$, the *dot product* or *scalar product*. This operates on two vectors giving a scalar result, thus

$$\boldsymbol{p} \cdot \boldsymbol{q} = (p_1, p_2, p_3) \cdot (q_1, q_2, q_3) = p_1 q_1 + p_2 q_2 + p_3 q_3$$

If the two vectors $\boldsymbol{p}$ and $\boldsymbol{q}$ are both in the form of direction cosines, that is, $|\boldsymbol{p}| = |\boldsymbol{q}| = 1$, and ψ is the angle between the lines defined by them, then $\boldsymbol{p} \cdot \boldsymbol{q} = \cos\psi$. Thus, in general, the angle between two directional vectors $\boldsymbol{p}$ and $\boldsymbol{q}$ (which meet at a point) is

$$\cos^{-1}\left(\frac{\boldsymbol{p} \cdot \boldsymbol{q}}{|\boldsymbol{p}||\boldsymbol{q}|}\right)$$

Obviously if $\boldsymbol{p}$ and $\boldsymbol{q}$ are mutually perpendicular directions then $\boldsymbol{p} \cdot \boldsymbol{q} = 0$.

The general point $\boldsymbol{x}$ on a plane is given by the vector equation

$$\boldsymbol{n} \cdot \boldsymbol{x} = k$$

where k is a scalar and $\boldsymbol{n}$ is the directional vector of the set of lines that are perpendicular to (or *normal* to) the plane (see example 5.2). If $\boldsymbol{a}$ is any given point on the plane then from the above equation we know that

$$\boldsymbol{n} \cdot \boldsymbol{a} = k$$

and thus, by replacing k, this equation may be rewritten as

$$\boldsymbol{n} \cdot \boldsymbol{x} = \boldsymbol{n} \cdot \boldsymbol{a} \quad \text{or} \quad \boldsymbol{n} \cdot (\boldsymbol{x} - \boldsymbol{a}) = 0$$

This latter fact is obvious from the property of the dot product just mentioned, namely that two mutually perpendicular lines have zero dot product. For any point $\boldsymbol{x}$ in the plane, $\boldsymbol{x} - \boldsymbol{a}$ may be considered as a direction vector of a line in the plane and, since $\boldsymbol{n}$ is normal to the plane and hence normal (that is, perpendicular) to every line in the plane, then $\boldsymbol{n} \cdot (\boldsymbol{x} - \boldsymbol{a}) = 0$.

Taking (x, y, z) as the general point on the plane with normal $\boldsymbol{n} \equiv (n_1, n_2, n_3)$, we obtain the usual coordinate representation of a plane

$$(n_1, n_2, n_3) \cdot (x, y, z) = n_1 x + n_2 y + n_3 z = k$$

THE POINT OF INTERSECTION OF A LINE AND A PLANE

Suppose the line is given by $\boldsymbol{b} + \mu\boldsymbol{d}$ and the plane by $\boldsymbol{n} \cdot \boldsymbol{x} = k$. Since the point of intersection is on both the line and plane we have to find the unique value of μ (if one exists) for which

$$\boldsymbol{n} \cdot (\boldsymbol{b} + \mu\boldsymbol{d}) = k$$

that is

$$\mu = \frac{k - \boldsymbol{n} \cdot \boldsymbol{b}}{\boldsymbol{n} \cdot \boldsymbol{d}}$$

provided $\boldsymbol{n} \cdot \boldsymbol{d} \neq 0$.

THE DISTANCE OF A PLANE FROM THE ORIGIN

To answer this question we first have to ask, 'what do we mean by the distance of a plane from a point p_1?' Common sense tells us that this is the distance from p_1 to the nearest point on the plane, p_2. Hence the normal from the plane at p_2 must pass through p_1 and the required distance is simply that between p_1 and p_2.

A line that passes through the origin and is normal to the plane $n \cdot x = k$ may be thought of as having the origin $0 = (0, 0, 0)$ as base vector, and directional vector n (that is, the line is $0 + \mu n$).

Hence the nearest point on the plane is

$$0 + \frac{(k - n \cdot 0)}{n \cdot n}\, n = \frac{kn}{|n|^2}$$

The distance of the origin from this point is $k/|n|$. Hence if n is given in the form of a direction cosine vector (that is, if $|n| = 1$), then k is seen to be the distance of the plane from the origin.

Example 5.2
Find the point of intersection of the line joining $(1, 2, 3)$ to $(1, 0, 1)$ with the plane $(2, 1, 2) \cdot x = 5$, and also the distance of the plane from the origin.

$b = (1, 2, 3), d = (1, 0, 1) - (1, 2, 3) = (0, -2, -2), n = (2, 1, 2)$

$n \cdot b = (2 \times 1 + 1 \times 2 + 2 \times 3) = 10$

$n \cdot d = (2 \times 0 + 1 \times -2 + 2 \times -2) = -6$

hence the point of intersection is

$$(1, 2, 3) + \frac{(5 - 10)}{-6}\,(0, -2, -2) = (1, 1/3, 4/3)$$

and the distance of the plane from the origin $= 5/|n| = 5/3$.

A program to solve such a problem is given below (program 5.2). Here vectors are stored as one-dimensional arrays whose indices lie between 1 and 3, corresponding to the x, y and z-coordinates respectively. The program reads in the plane information K and N(3), and the line information, base vector B(3) and directional vector D(3). A function DOT is used to calculate the dot product of two vectors.

```
      FUNCTION DOT(P,Q)
C FUNCTION TO FIND THE DOT PRODUCT OF TWO VECTORS P AND Q.
      DIMENSION P(3),Q(3)
      DOT=P(1)*Q(1)+P(2)*Q(2)+P(3)*Q(3)
      RETURN
      END
```

Program 5.1

Since we are working with REAL numbers, with all their attendant rounding error problems, we cannot check whether the dot product is zero, instead we see whether its value is sufficiently small to be considered zero (and what is meant by sufficiently small is left to the programmer).

```
C PROGRAM TO FIND THE POINT OF INTERSECTION PT OF A LINE
C B + RMU*D  AND A PLANE    N.X = K . B,D,N,X,PT ARE VECTORS.
      REAL B(3),D(3),N(3),PT(3),K
      READ(5,*) K,N,B,D
      DOT1=DOT(N,D)
C IF LINE AND PLANE ARE PARALLEL THEN STOP.
      IF(ABS(DOT1).LT.0.000001) STOP
      RMU=(K-DOT(N,B))/DOT1
      DO 1 I=1,3
      PT(I)=B(I)+RMU*D(I)
    1 CONTINUE
```

Program 5.2

THE POINT OF INTERSECTION OF TWO LINES

Of course the two lines have to be coplanar and non-parallel for there to be a real point of intersection; however, there is no need to check these facts independently — 'it will all come out in the wash'. Suppose the lines are $b_1 + \mu d_1$ and $b_2 + \lambda d_2$ for all real values of μ and λ. We have to fix unique values for μ and λ such that

$$b_1 + \mu d_1 = b_2 + \lambda d_2$$

Hence, we have three equations in two unknowns (one equation per coordinate). Thus, for this problem to make sense, one of the equations must be redundant, that is, one equation must be a combination of the other two. If this is not the case, then the lines are not coplanar. If all three are similar, that is, each is a multiple of every other, then the lines are parallel. Hence the question reduces to one of finding two non-similar equations (if possible), solving them for μ and λ and then checking that this solution also satisfies the remaining equation.

Example 5.3
Find the point of intersection (if any) of

(a) $(1, 1, 1) + \mu(2, 1, 3)$ with $(0, 0, 1) + \lambda(-1, 1, 1)$
(b) $(2, 3, 4) + \mu(1, 1, 1)$ with $(-2, -3, -4) + \lambda(1, 2, 3)$

In (a) the three equations are

$$1 + 2\mu = 0 - \lambda \tag{5.4}$$

$$1 + \mu = 0 + \lambda \tag{5.5}$$

$$1 + 3\mu = 1 + \lambda \tag{5.6}$$

From equations 5.4 and 5.5 we get $\mu = -2/3$ and $\lambda = 1/3$, which when substituted into equation 5.6 give $1 + 3(-2/3)$ on the left-hand side and $1 + 1(1/3)$ on the right, which are obviously unequal; thus the lines do not intersect.

From (b) we get the equations

$$2 + \mu = -2 + \lambda \qquad\qquad (5.7)$$

$$3 + \mu = -3 + 2\lambda \qquad\qquad (5.8)$$

$$4 + \mu = -4 + 3\lambda \qquad\qquad (5.9)$$

From equations 5.7 and 5.8 we get $\mu = -2$ and $\lambda = 2$, and these values satisfy equation 5.9; hence the point of intersection is

$$(2, 3, 4) + -2(1, 1, 1) = (-2, -3, -4) + 2(1, 2, 3) = (0, 1, 2)$$

Exercise 5.1

Program this problem, remembering that we are working with REAL numbers, so when it is time to check the solution with the remaining equation, we cannot expect equality; check only that the difference between the left- and right-hand sides is sufficiently small.

Note that if the two independent equations are

$$a_{11}\mu + a_{12}\lambda = b_1$$

$$a_{21}\mu + a_{22}\lambda = b_2$$

then the determinant of this pair of equations $D = a_{11}a_{22} - a_{12}a_{21}$ will be non-zero, and we have the solutions

$$\mu = (a_{22}b_1 - a_{12}b_2)/D \quad \text{and} \quad \lambda = (a_{11}b_2 - a_{21}b_1)/D$$

We now introduce a new vector operator, that is, the *vector product* **x** , which operates on two vectors p and q, giving a vector result as follows

$$p \times q = (p_1, p_2, p_3) \times (q_1, q_2, q_3)$$

$$= (p_2q_3 - p_3q_2, p_3q_1 - p_1q_3, p_1q_2 - p_2q_1)$$

If p and q are directional vectors (not parallel) then $p \times q$ is the directional vector perpendicular to both p and q. It should be noted that $p \times q \neq q \times p$; these two vectors specify the same direction but they are of opposite senses, for example, $(1, 0, 0) \times (0, 1, 0) = (0, 0, 1)$ but $(0, 1, 0) \times (1, 0, 0) = (0, 0, -1)$; while $(0, 0, 1)$ and $(0, 0, -1)$ are both directions parallel to the z-axis, the first is in the sense of the positive z-direction, and the second in the negative.

A subroutine VECPROD, which produces the vector product R(3) of two vectors P(3) and Q(3), is given below.

```
      SUBROUTINE VECPROD(P,Q,R)
C ROUTINE TO CALCULATE R, THE VECTOR PRODUCT OF TWO VECTORS P AND Q.
      DIMENSION P(3),Q(3),R(3)
      DO 1 I=1,3
      I1=MOD(I,3)+1
      I2=MOD(I1,3)+1
      R(I)=P(I1)*Q(I2)-P(I2)*Q(I1)
    1 CONTINUE
      RETURN
      END
```

Program 5.3

THE PLANE THROUGH THREE GIVEN NON-COLLINEAR POINTS

Suppose the three given points are p_1, p_2 and p_3. Then $p_2 - p_1$ and $p_3 - p_1$ are vectors which define directions of two different lines in the plane, the lines being coincident at p_1. The first line goes through p_2 and the second through p_3. We know that the normal to the plane is perpendicular to every line in that plane, and thus in particular to the lines with directions $p_2 - p_1$ and $p_3 - p_1$. Hence, since the lines are not parallel, $p_2 - p_1 \neq p_3 - p_1$, the normal direction must be $(p_2 - p_1) \times (p_3 - p_1)$, and since the plane obviously contains the point p_1, we may take the general equation of this plane to be

$$((p_2 - p_1) \times (p_3 - p_1)) \cdot (x - p_1) = 0$$

Example 5.4
Find the plane through points $(0, 1, 1), (1, 2, 3)$ and $(-2, 3, -1)$ in coordinate form.

This is given by the general point $x \equiv (x, y, z)$

$$(((1, 2, 3) - (0, 1, 1)) \times ((-2, 3, -1) - (0, 1, 1))) \cdot ((x, y, z) - (0, 1, 1)) = 0$$

that is

$$((1, 1, 2) \times (-2, 2, -2)) \cdot (x, y - 1, z - 1) = 0$$

that is

$$(-6, -2, 4) \cdot (x, y - 1, z - 1) = 0$$

Hence the plane is given by the equation $-6x - 2y + 4z = 2$ or in the equivalent form $3x + y - 2z = -1$.

THE POINT OF INTERSECTION OF THREE PLANES

We assume that the three planes are given by the vector equations 5.10 to 5.12 below. The point of intersection of the three planes must thus lie in each plane and hence satisfy all three equations

$$n_1 \cdot x = k_1 \tag{5.10}$$

$$n_2 \cdot x = k_2 \tag{5.11}$$

$$n_3 \cdot x = k_3 \tag{5.12}$$

where $n_1 \equiv (n_{11}, n_{12}, n_{13})$, $n_2 \equiv (n_{21}, n_{22}, n_{23})$ and $n_3 \equiv (n_{31}, n_{32}, n_{33})$. These three equations can be replaced by the matrix equation

$$\begin{pmatrix} n_{11} & n_{12} & n_{13} \\ n_{21} & n_{22} & n_{23} \\ n_{31} & n_{32} & n_{33} \end{pmatrix} \times \begin{pmatrix} x \\ y \\ z \end{pmatrix} = \begin{pmatrix} k_1 \\ k_2 \\ k_3 \end{pmatrix}$$

and so the solution for x is given by the column vector

$$\begin{pmatrix} x \\ y \\ z \end{pmatrix} = \begin{pmatrix} n_{11} & n_{12} & n_{13} \\ n_{21} & n_{22} & n_{23} \\ n_{31} & n_{32} & n_{33} \end{pmatrix}^{-1} \times \begin{pmatrix} k_1 \\ k_2 \\ k_3 \end{pmatrix}$$

So any program requiring the intersection of three planes necessarily uses the inverse of a 3 x 3 matrix; we could use a computer package to solve this problem, but it is much simpler to write our own routine. Subroutine INV uses the Adjoint method to find NI, the inverse of the REAL 3 x 3 matrix N.

```
      SUBROUTINE INV(N,NI)
C CALCULATE MATRIX NI, THE INVERSE OF MATRIX N BY THE ADJOINT METHOD.
C N IS ASSUMED TO BE A REAL NONSINGULAR MATRIX.
      REAL N(3,3),NI(3,3)
C FIND DET, THE DETERMINANT OF MATRIX N.
      DET=N(1,1)*(N(2,2)*N(3,3)-N(2,3)*N(3,2))  +
     +     N(1,2)*(N(2,3)*N(3,1)-N(2,1)*N(3,3))  +
     +     N(1,3)*(N(2,1)*N(3,2)-N(2,2)*N(3,1))
C THE INVERSE IS THE ADJOINT MATRIX DIVIDED BY THE DETERMINANT.
      DO 2 I=1,3
      I1=MOD(I,3)+1
      I2=MOD(I1,3)+1
      DO 1 J=1,3
      J1=MOD(J,3)+1
      J2=MOD(J1,3)+1
      NI(J,I)=(N(I1,J1)*N(I2,J2)-N(I1,J2)*N(I2,J1))/DET
    1 CONTINUE
    2 CONTINUE
      RETURN
      END
```

Program 5.4

As usual, vectors are represented in programs by one-dimensional arrays, thus PT(3) will contain the solution of the equation, x; K(3) will be the column vector of plane constants. We are given the normals of the planes n_1, n_2 and n_3 in the form of a two-dimensional array N(3, 3). So the value of x is found by the following code.

```
C PROGRAM TO FIND PT, THE POINT OF INTERSECTION OF THE THREE
C PLANES   N(I, ).X = K(I) ; I=1,2 OR 3.
C N(I, ) REPRESENTS THE NORMAL TO THE I'TH PLANE, (N(I,1),N(I,2),N(I,3)).
      REAL N(3,3),NI(3,3),K(3),PT(3)
      READ(5,*) N,K
      CALL INV(N,NI)
C THE COLUMN VECTOR PT IS THE PRODUCT OF THE INVERSE MATRIX NI
C AND THE COLUMN VECTOR K.
      DO 2 I=1,3
      PTI=0.0
      DO 1 J=1,3
      PTI=PTI+NI(I,J)*K(J)
    1 CONTINUE
      PT(I)=PTI
    2 CONTINUE
```

Program 5.5

Obviously if any two of the planes are parallel, then DET, the determinant of the matrix N, is zero and the inverse does not exist, and incidently our program would fail.

Example 5.5
Find the point of intersection of the three planes $(0, 1, 1) \cdot x = 2, (1, 2, 3) \cdot x = 4$ and $(1, 1, 1) \cdot x = 0$

In the matrix form we have

$$\begin{pmatrix} 0 & 1 & 1 \\ 1 & 2 & 3 \\ 1 & 1 & 1 \end{pmatrix} \times \begin{pmatrix} x \\ y \\ z \end{pmatrix} = \begin{pmatrix} 2 \\ 4 \\ 0 \end{pmatrix}$$

The inverse of

$$\begin{pmatrix} 0 & 1 & 1 \\ 1 & 2 & 3 \\ 1 & 1 & 1 \end{pmatrix}$$

is

$$\begin{pmatrix} -1 & 0 & 1 \\ 2 & -1 & 1 \\ -1 & 1 & -1 \end{pmatrix}$$

and

$$\begin{pmatrix} x \\ y \\ z \end{pmatrix} = \begin{pmatrix} -1 & 0 & 1 \\ 2 & -1 & 1 \\ -1 & 1 & -1 \end{pmatrix} \times \begin{pmatrix} 2 \\ 4 \\ 0 \end{pmatrix} = \begin{pmatrix} -2 \\ 0 \\ 2 \end{pmatrix}$$

This solution is easily checked

$(0, 1, 1) \cdot (-2, 0, 2) = 2 \qquad (1, 2, 3) \cdot (-2, 0, 2) = 4$ and $(1, 1, 1) \cdot (-2, 0, 2) = 0$

and thus the point $(-2, 0, 2)$ lies on all three planes and so is their point of intersection.

THE LINE COMMON TO TWO PLANES

Let the two planes be

$$p \cdot x = k_1 \quad \text{and} \quad q \cdot x = k_2$$

Since we naturally assume that the planes are not parallel $p \neq \lambda q$ for all λ. The common line is in the first plane and hence it must be perpendicular to the normal to that plane, p (p is perpendicular to every line in the plane); it must also be perpendicular to q for the same reason. But we know that a line perpendicular to two non-equal directional vectors p and q has direction $p \times q$. Thus the line must be of the form

$$b + \mu(p \times q)$$

where b is any point on the line. In order completely to classify the line we must find one such b. Why not take the point that is the point of intersection of the two planes with a third which is not parallel to the former? Choosing a plane with normal $p \times q$ will satisfy this condition, and we have already calculated this vector product! Thus the third plane is in the form $(p \times q) \cdot x = k_3$. Of course this plane still requires a value for k_3; why not assume that the plane goes through the origin and thus $k_3 = 0$, and b is given by the column vector

$$b = \begin{pmatrix} p_1 & p_2 & p_3 \\ q_1 & q_2 & q_3 \\ p_2 q_3 - p_3 q_2 & p_3 q_1 - p_1 q_3 & p_1 q_2 - p_2 q_1 \end{pmatrix}^{-1} \times \begin{pmatrix} k_1 \\ k_2 \\ 0 \end{pmatrix}$$

Example 5.6
Find the line common to the planes $(0, 1, 1) \cdot x = 2$ and $(1, 2, 3) \cdot x = 2$.

$p = (0, 1, 1)$ and $q = (1, 2, 3)$, and so $p \times q = (1 \times 3 - 1 \times 2, 1 \times 1 - 0 \times 3, 0 \times 2 - 1 \times 1) = (1, 1, -1)$. And we require the inverse of

$$\begin{pmatrix} 0 & 1 & 1 \\ 1 & 2 & 3 \\ 1 & 1 & -1 \end{pmatrix}$$

that is

$$\frac{1}{3}\begin{pmatrix} -5 & 2 & 1 \\ 4 & -1 & 1 \\ -1 & 1 & -1 \end{pmatrix}$$

and hence the point of intersection of the three planes (the required base vector) is

$$\frac{1}{3}\begin{pmatrix} -5 & 2 & 1 \\ 4 & -1 & 1 \\ -1 & 1 & -1 \end{pmatrix} \times \begin{pmatrix} 2 \\ 2 \\ 0 \end{pmatrix} = \frac{1}{3}\begin{pmatrix} -6 \\ 6 \\ 0 \end{pmatrix} = \begin{pmatrix} -2 \\ 2 \\ 0 \end{pmatrix}$$

and the line is $(-2, 2, 0) + \mu(1, 1, -1)$.

It is easy to check that this line lies in both planes because

$$(0, 1, 1) \cdot ((-2, 2, 0) + \mu(1, 1, -1)) = (0, 1, 1) \cdot (-2, 2, 0)$$
$$+ (0, 1, 1) \cdot \mu(1, 1, -1) = 2$$

$$(1, 2, 3) \cdot ((-2, 2, 0) + \mu(1, 1, -1)) = (1, 2, 3) \cdot (-2, 2, 0)$$
$$+ (1, 2, 3) \cdot \mu(1, 1, -1) = 2$$

The program to solve this problem is given below, and as we can see it is very similar to the last program segment.

```
C PROGRAM TO FIND  B + RMU*D , THE LINE COMMON TO TWO PLANES
C P.X = K(1)    AND Q.X = K(2) .
      REAL N(3,3),NI(3,3),B(3),D(3),P(3),Q(3),K(3)
      READ(5,*) P,Q,K
C D, THE DIRECTIONAL VECTOR OF THE LINE IS THE VECTOR PRODUCT OF P AND Q.
      CALL VECPROD(P,Q,D)
C CREATE A NEW PLANE AND PUT NORMALS TO THE THREE PLANES IN MATRIX N.
C THE CONSTANT OF THE NEW PLANE IS ZERO.
      K(3)=0.0
      DO 1 I=1,3
      N(1,I)=P(I)
      N(2,I)=Q(I)
      N(3,I)=D(I)
    1 CONTINUE
C B, THE BASE POINT OF THE LINE IS THE POINT OF INTERSECTION OF
C THE THREE PLANES.
      CALL INV(N,NI)
      DO 3 I=1,3
      BI=0.0
      DO 2 J=1,3
      BI=BI+NI(I,J)*K(J)
    2 CONTINUE
      B(I)=BI
    3 CONTINUE
```

Program 5.6

In the routine to find the inverse of a matrix we had to calculate the determinant of the matrix, DET. The matrix in the last example is in a very special form, and so we recalculate DET

$$\begin{aligned}
\mathrm{DET} &= p_1(p_1q_2{}^2 - p_2q_1q_2 + p_1q_3{}^2 - p_3q_1q_3) \\
&\quad + p_2(p_2q_3{}^2 - p_3q_2q_3 + p_2q_1{}^2 - p_1q_2q_1) \\
&\quad + p_3(p_3q_1{}^2 - p_1q_3q_1 + p_3q_2{}^2 - p_2q_3q_2) \\
&= p_1{}^2(q_2{}^2 + q_3{}^2) + p_2{}^2(q_3{}^2 + q_2{}^2) + p_3{}^2(q_1{}^2 + q_2{}^2) - 2\sum_{i<j} p_ip_jq_iq_j \\
&= (p_1{}^2 + p_2{}^2 + p_3{}^2)(q_1{}^2 + q_2{}^2 + q_3{}^2) - p_1{}^2q_1{}^2 - p_2{}^2q_2{}^2 - p_3{}^2q_3{}^2 \\
&\quad - 2\sum_{i<j} p_ip_jq_iq_j \\
&= (p_1{}^2 + p_2{}^2 + p_3{}^2)(q_1{}^2 + q_2{}^2 + q_3{}^2) - (p_1q_1 + p_2q_2 + p_3q_3)^2 \\
&= (p \cdot p)(q \cdot q) - (p \cdot q)^2
\end{aligned}$$

If p and q are direction cosine vectors then $p \cdot p$ and $q \cdot q$ are both equal to 1 and hence the determinant is simply $1 - (p \cdot q)^2$, a much simpler calculation. This new interpretation of DET is also instructive, since $p \cdot q$ is the cosine of the angle ψ between the two lines, then DET $= 1 - \cos^2 \psi = \sin^2 \psi$. This shows the real meaning of the determinant — it is the square of the area of the parallelogram formed by vectors p and q, and in general it is the volume of the solid formed by the three vectors.

THE FUNCTIONAL REPRESENTATION OF A SURFACE

We have already seen the simplest form of surface, namely a plane

$$n_1 x + n_2 y + n_3 z - k = 0$$

The function $f(x, y, z) \equiv n_1 x + n_2 y + n_3 z - k$, a simple linear polynomial in x, y and z, can be used to define this surface; it also enables us to divide space into two parts. For all points (x, y, z) such that $f(x, y, z) = 0$ lie on the surface, those with $f(x, y, z) > 0$ lie in one part and those with $f(x, y, z) < 0$ lie in the other. This fact is true for any surface that divides space into two parts, for example, $f(x, y, z) \equiv r^2 - x^2 - y^2 - z^2$ defines a sphere with radius r. If $f(x, y, z) > 0$ then the point (x, y, z) lies inside the sphere, and $f(x, y, z) < 0$ lies outside the sphere. This fact is very useful because there are many instances when we wish to know whether two points $p \equiv (p_1, p_2, p_3)$ and $q \equiv (q_1, q_2, q_3)$, say, lie on the same side of a surface or not (especially when considering Hidden Line Algorithms, chapter 8). All we need to do is to check whether the sign of $f(p_1, p_2, p_3)$ is the same as $f(q_1, q_2, q_3)$. If they have opposite signs then all line segments joining them must intersect the surface.

IS A POINT ON THE SAME SIDE OF A PLANE AS THE ORIGIN?

Suppose that the plane is defined by three points (non-collinear), p_1, p_2 and p_3, and the given point is e; we assume that neither e nor the origin lie in the plane. We know from earlier theory that the plane is given by

$$((p_2 - p_1) \times (p_3 - p_1)) \cdot (x - p_1) = 0$$

This is in fact the functional representation of the plane, that is

$$f(x, y, z) = f(x) = ((p_2 - p_1) \times (p_2 - p_1)) \cdot (x - p_1)$$

and all we need to do is to compare the value of $f(e)$ with $f(0)$

Example 5.7
Is $(1, 1, 3)$ on the same side of the plane formed by $(0, 1, 1)$, $(1, 2, 3)$ and $(-2, 3, -1)$ as the origin $(0, 0, 0)$?

From example 5.4 we know that the plane is

$$(-6, -2, 4) \cdot (x - (0, 1, 1)) = 0$$

and hence

$$f(x) = (-6, -2, 4) \cdot (x - (0, 1, 1))$$

Thus

$$f(0, 0, 0) = -(-6, -2, 4) \cdot (0, 1, 1) = -2$$

and

$$f(1, 1, 3) = (-6, -2, 4) \cdot ((1, 1, 3) - (0, 1, 1)) = 2$$

Hence $(1, 1, 3)$ is on the opposite side of the plane to the origin.

This, and all the other examples given in this chapter, were taken out of the context of computer graphics, and hence may seem rather contrived. However, we shall see that the techniques given in this chapter are invaluable when dealing with drawing objects in three-dimensional space. Obviously, since we are restricted to the two dimensions of the graphics screen, we may not draw any sensible representations of three-dimensional space until we have dealt with projecting images of objects in three dimensions into the lower dimension. This is not the only reason that there were no diagrams in the chapter — they were deliberately left out. It is essential to have confidence in the mathematical representations of points, lines, planes and surfaces, and so we have relied totally on the vector notation and refrained from running to diagrams for help. Only practice will lead to the necessary understanding of manipulating these three-dimensional objects. It is left to the reader to generate exercises related to this chapter; after all, it has been shown that it is very easy to check whether solutions to problems are correct.

6 Matrix Transformation of Three-dimensional Space; Orthographic Projections

Before we consider projections of three-dimensional space on to our necessarily two-dimensional screen, we need to introduce the concepts of transforming coordinate systems (as we did with two-dimensional space in chapter 3). As in the two-dimensional case there are three basic transformations: change of origin, change of scale and rotation of axes. Since we have introduced the idea of matrix representation of transformations in this lower dimension, we shall move directly to a similar representation of three-dimensional space. As in the earlier case, the square matrices representing the transformations will be one dimension greater than space, that is, 4 x 4, and a general point in space relative to some coordinate triad (x, y, z) is represented by the column vector

$$\begin{pmatrix} x \\ y \\ z \\ 1 \end{pmatrix}$$

We start with our library of routines for three-dimensional transformations. In the programs Tx is TX, etc.

TRANSLATION OF ORIGIN

If the origin of the new coordinate triad is the point (Tx, Ty, Tz) in the old system, then the general point (x, y, z) will be transformed to $(x - Tx, y - Ty, z - Tz)$ in the new system. Necessarily (Tx, Ty, Tz) becomes $(0, 0, 0)$ in the new triad of axes. Hence the matrix to represent this transformation (remembering that we premultiply the column vector point by the matrix) is

$$\begin{pmatrix} 1 & 0 & 0 & -Tx \\ 0 & 1 & 0 & -Ty \\ 0 & 0 & 1 & -Tz \\ 0 & 0 & 0 & 1 \end{pmatrix}$$

and the routine for producing such a matrix is given by the subroutine TRAN.

```
      SUBROUTINE TRAN(TX,TY,TZ,A)
C CALCULATE 3-D AXES TRANSLATION MATRIX.
      DIMENSION A(4,4)
      DO 2 I=1,4
      DO 1 J=1,4
      A(I,J)=0.0
    1 CONTINUE
      A(I,I)=1.0
    2 CONTINUE
      A(1,4)=-TX
      A(2,4)=-TY
      A(3,4)=-TZ
      RETURN
      END
```

Program 6.1

CHANGE OF SCALE

If the point $(1, 1, 1)$ in the old coordinate system is changed to (Sx, Sy, Sz) in the new system, then the general point (x, y, z) of the old changes to $(x \times Sx, y \times Sy, z \times Sz)$ and the matrix to achieve this is

$$\begin{pmatrix} Sx & 0 & 0 & 0 \\ 0 & Sy & 0 & 0 \\ 0 & 0 & Sz & 0 \\ 0 & 0 & 0 & 1 \end{pmatrix}$$

and the subroutine SCALE is used to obtain this matrix.

```
      SUBROUTINE SCALE(SX,SY,SZ,A)
C CALCULATE 3-D AXES SCALING MATRIX.
      DIMENSION A(4,4)
      DO 2 I=1,4
      DO 1 J=1,4
      A(I,J)=0.0
    1 CONTINUE
    2 CONTINUE
      A(1,1)=SX
      A(2,2)=SY
      A(3,3)=SZ
      A(4,4)=1.0
      RETURN
      END
```

Program 6.2

ROTATION OF COORDINATE AXES

Initially we consider the simplest cases, where the axis of rotation is coincident with one of the coordinate axes; later we shall consider rotation about a general axis. Thus we have three cases to consider.

Rotation by an Angle θ about the z-axis

Referring to figure 6.1a, the axis of rotation is perpendicular to the page (the

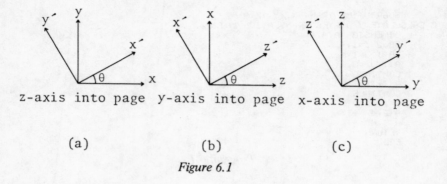

(a)   (b)   (c)

Figure 6.1

positive z-axis is into the page), and, since we are using left-handed axes, the figure shows the case where the remaining axes (x and y) rotate through an angle θ.

We have thus reduced the problem to a rotation in two-dimensional space and, referring to chapter 3, we see that a point (x, y, z) in the old system becomes (x', y', z') in the new system, where

$$x' = x \cos \theta + y \sin \theta$$

$$y' = -x \sin \theta + y \cos \theta$$

$$z' = z$$

and hence the required matrix is

$$\begin{pmatrix} \cos \theta & \sin \theta & 0 & 0 \\ -\sin \theta & \cos \theta & 0 & 0 \\ 0 & 0 & 1 & 0 \\ 0 & 0 & 0 & 1 \end{pmatrix}$$

Rotation by an Angle θ about the y-axis

Since we are using left-handed axes and the positive y-axis is into the page (figure 6.1b) then, if the positive z-axis is horizontal and to the right of the origin, the positive x-axis is vertical and above the origin. (This notation must be adhered to or we will find that we have inadvertently rotated through an angle $-\theta$ instead of θ.) If (x, y, z) in the old system becomes (x', y', z') in the new then

$$z' = z \cos \theta + x \sin \theta$$

$$x' = -z \sin \theta + x \cos \theta$$

$$y' = y$$

and the matrix is

$$\begin{pmatrix} \cos\theta & 0 & -\sin\theta & 0 \\ 0 & 1 & 0 & 0 \\ \sin\theta & 0 & \cos\theta & 0 \\ 0 & 0 & 0 & 1 \end{pmatrix}$$

Rotation by an Angle θ about the x-axis

In a similar manner we find that if (x, y, z) is transformed to (x', y', z') then
(figure 6.1c)

$$y' = y\cos\theta + z\sin\theta$$

$$z' = -y\sin\theta + z\cos\theta$$

$$x' = x$$

and the matrix is

$$\begin{pmatrix} 1 & 0 & 0 & 0 \\ 0 & \cos\theta & \sin\theta & 0 \\ 0 & -\sin\theta & \cos\theta & 0 \\ 0 & 0 & 0 & 1 \end{pmatrix}$$

To produce A, any one of these three matrices, we describe a subroutine
ROT(M, THETA, A), where THETA is the angle of rotation (in radians) and M
is an index used to specify the axis of rotation (M = 1 specifies the x-axis, M = 2
the y-axis and M = 3 the z-axis).

```
      SUBROUTINE ROT(M,THETA,A)
C CALCULATE 3-D AXES ROTATION MATRIX A ABOUT DIRECTION M
C M=1  X-AXIS  M=2  Y-AXIS   M=3  Z-AXIS.
      DIMENSION A(4,4)
      DO 2 I=1,4
      DO 1 J=1,4
      A(I,J)=0.0
    1 CONTINUE
    2 CONTINUE
      A(4,4)=1.0
      A(M,M)=1.0
      M1=MOD(M,3)+1
      M2=MOD(M1,3)+1
      C=COS(THETA)
      S=SIN(THETA)
      A(M1,M1)=C
      A(M2,M2)=C
      A(M1,M2)=S
      A(M2,M1)=-S
      RETURN
      END
```

Program 6.3

COMBINING TRANSFORMATIONS

As with the two-dimensional case, we shall combine sequences of such transformations and hence require a routine to multiply two matrices A and B giving the product matrix C. *Remember* that we are premultiplying the matrices and so the right-hand matrix B refers to the initial transformation, and the left-hand matrix A refers to the second transformation. Also note that matrix multiplication is non-commutative: $A \times B$ is not necessarily equal to $B \times A$.

```
      SUBROUTINE MULT(A,B,C)
C 4X4 MATRIX PRODUCT.
      DIMENSION A(4,4),B(4,4),C(4,4)
      DO 1 I=1,4
      DO 2 J=1,4
      AB=0.0
      DO 3 K=1,4
      AB=AB+A(I,K)*B(K,J)
    3 CONTINUE
      C(I,J)=AB
    2 CONTINUE
    1 CONTINUE
      RETURN
      END
```

Program 6.4

INVERSE TRANSFORMATIONS

Naturally, for all three types of transformation (translation, scale and rotation), there will be an inverse transformation that would restore the axes to their original position. The matrix form of the inverse transformation of a given transformation (matrix A, say) is logically the inverse matrix of A, A^{-1} (AM, say). There is no need to calculate directly such an inverse using a subroutine similar to INV (chapter 5). If A is a translation matrix, the A and AM are found by the subroutine calls

CALL TRAN(TX, TY, TZ, A)

CALL TRAN(−TX, −TY, −TZ, AM)

Similarly if A is a scaling matrix we get

CALL SCALE (SX, SY, SZ, A)

CALL SCALE(1.0/SX, 1.0/SY, 1.0/SZ, AM)

If A is a rotation matrix we have

CALL ROT(M, THETA, A)

CALL ROT(M, −THETA, AM)

If a transformation T is given by a sequence of elementary transformations $A_1, \ldots, A_n$ (that is, $T = A_n \times A_{n-1} \times \ldots \times A_1$; note the order) then the inverse transformation T^{-1} is necessarily

$$T^{-1} = A_1^{-1} \times A_2^{-1} \times \ldots \ldots \times A_{n-1}^{-1} \times A_n^{-1}$$

($T^{-1} \times T = I$, the identity matrix). It cannot be overstressed that the order of the A_is and A_i^{-1}s ($i = 1, 2, \ldots, n$) is important: matrix multiplication is non-commutative!

TRANSFORMATION OF SPACE

As with the two-dimensional case, some people find it easier to visualise keeping the axes fixed and moving the whole of space relative to these axes instead. Again we will see that the result will be equivalent to transformations of axes.

Linear transformation

Space is moved by a vector (Tx, Ty, Tz), so that the general point (x, y, z) is moved to $(x + Tx, y + Tz, z + Tz)$ relative to the same fixed coordinate triad. This is the same as keeping space fixed and moving the coordinate origin to the point $(-Tx, -Ty, -Tz)$.

Stretching space

If space is expanded by a factor Sx in the x-direction, Sy in the y-direction and Sz in the z-direction (all relative to a fixed origin and axes), this is equivalent to changing the scale of axes so that the point $(1, 1, 1)$ becomes (Sx, Sy, Sz).

Rotation of Space

If space is rotated about a given axis through the origin by an angle θ, then this is equivalent to rotating the coordinates axes about the same axis by an angle $-\theta$.

ORTHOGRAPHIC PROJECTIONS

Having introduced a number of ways of manipulating space relative to a triad of axes (or vice versa), we should now consider how to draw objects in such a three-dimensional space before giving examples of these transformations. Obviously we are limited to a two-dimensional graphics screen, and hence have to consider ways of projecting space (or more precisely objects in space) on to the screen (or the plane of a microfilm plotter, etc.). We assume that all objects are defined relative to a fixed triad of axes — the ABSOLUTE triad, whose origin, x and y-axes are identified with the screen origin and the horizontal and vertical directions, respectively. The *z*-axis is perpendicular to the plane of the screen; the positive *z*-axis is behind the plane. The simplest method of projecting objects defined in this triad on to the screen is simply to ignore the *z*-coordinates of every point in space — the *z*-orthographic projection. Thus a point (x, y, z) in the ABSOLUTE triad is projected on to the point (x, y) in the screen coordinate system. The projection of a line (defined by its end points) is the line joining the corresponding projected points on the screen. Thus a cube with eight corners $(\pm 1, \pm 1, \pm 1)$ will appear on the screen as a square with four corners $(\pm 1, \pm 1)$.

A cube need not be in this elementary form; it could be centred at a point other than the origin, and in a peculiar orientation. We thus have to get the data for such objects into a program. There are many objects which may be defined in a very simple form (relative to what we will call the SETUP triad of axes) by a call to a subroutine SETUP and the use of BLOCK DATA. This enables the simple form of data to be stored in labelled COMMON stores /VERTS/ and /LINES/. A cube SETUP is given below.

```
      SUBROUTINE SETUP
C SETUP THE VERTEX AND LINE INFORMATION FOR A CUBE.
      COMMON/VERTS/NOV,X(300),Y(300),Z(300),XP(300),YP(300)
      COMMON/LINES/NOL,LINV(2,400)
      NOV=8
      NOL=12
      RETURN
      END


      BLOCK DATA CUBE
      COMMON/VERTS/NOV,X(300),Y(300),Z(300),XP(300),YP(300)
      COMMON/LINES/NOL,LINV(2,400)
C X,Y,Z COORDINATES OF CUBE OF SIDE 2, CENTRED ON THE ORIGIN.
      DATA X/1.0,1.0,1.0,1.0,-1.0,-1.0,-1.0,-1.0/
      DATA Y/1.0,1.0,-1.0,-1.0,1.0,1.0,-1.0,-1.0/
      DATA Z/1.0,-1.0,1.0,-1.0,1.0,-1.0,1.0,-1.0/
C PAIRS OF VERTEX INDICES WHICH FORM THE END POINTS OF THE LINES.
      DATA LINV/1,2,2,4,4,3,3,1,5,6,6,8,8,7,7,5,1,5,2,6,3,7,4,8/
      END
```

Program 6.5

Each vertex of the figure is given a unique index, and the *x*, *y* and *z*-coordinates of the Ith vertex are stored in X(I), Y(I) and Z(I), respectively. There will be NOV vertices in total (there is storage space for 300); we do not limit ourselves to the actual number (eight in the case of the cube) because we wish to make the programs that follow as general as possible. Thus we may change figures (to a tetrahedron, cuboctahedron, etc. — see below) with a minimum of disruption. There is also room for 400 lines; there will be NOL in total (for a cube, NOL = 12), and the Jth line is stored as a pair of integers LINV(1, J) and LINV(2, J), the indices of the vertices at the end of the Jth line.

To find the ACTUAL coordinates of the figure, that is, the coordinates relative to an arbitrary but fixed ACTUAL triad, we need to define the relationship between the SETUP and ACTUAL coordinate systems. This is achieved by a call to a subroutine ACTUAL(*P*), which returns the matrix *P* describing the transformation between the triads. Hence in the program that follows, if we wish to use the same SETUP figure but a different ACTUAL coordinate system, all we need to do is to change the ACTUAL subroutine. (We give a number of such routines.)

We may then identify the ACTUAL triad with the ABSOLUTE triad of the graphics screen and produce a z-orthographic projection. Since the z-coordinates will be ignored by this projection, only the x and y-coordinates of the projected points are stored — in the XP and YP arrays. These are joined in the correct order, using the information in the LINV array.

```
C PROGRAM TO DRAW ORTHOGRAPHIC PROJECTION OF AN OBJECT.
      COMMON/VERTS/NOV,X(300),Y(300),Z(300),XP(300),YP(300)
      COMMON/LINES/NOL,LINV(2,400)
      DIMENSION P(4,4),Q(4,4),R(4,4)
C SETUP COORDINATES AND LINES WHICH DEFINE THE OBJECT.
      CALL SETUP
C CALCULATE THE SETUP TO ACTUAL MATRIX P AND THE ACTUAL TO OBSERVER
C MATRIX Q. THE SETUP TO OBSERVER MATRIX R IS THUS Q X P .
      CALL ACTUAL(P)
      CALL OBSERVE(Q)
      CALL MULT(Q,P,R)
C TRANSFORM THE OBJECT USING R AND STORE THE X AND Y COORDINATES
C IN THE XP AND YP ARRAYS FOR THE ORTHOGRAPHIC PROJECTION.
      DO 1 I=1,NOV
      XP(I)=R(1,1)*X(I)+R(1,2)*Y(I)+R(1,3)*Z(I)+R(1,4)
      YP(I)=R(2,1)*X(I)+R(2,2)*Y(I)+R(2,3)*Z(I)+R(2,4)
C NO NEED TO CALCULATE Z-COORDINATE.
    1 CONTINUE
      CALL START(2)
      CALL PLOT(9.5,7.375,-3)
C NOW PLOT THE LINE SEGMENTS OF THE ORTHOGRAPHIC PROJECTION.
      DO 2 I=1,NOL
      I1=LINV(1,I)
      I2=LINV(2,I)
      CALL PLOT(XP(I1),YP(I1),3)
      CALL PLOT(XP(I2),YP(I2),2)
    2 CONTINUE
```

Program 6.6

Ignore the call to the OBSERVE subroutine; imagine that it returns the identity matrix. It will be explained later. The following example illustrates these ideas.

Example 6.1
Draw the z-orthographic projection of a cube (a transparent 'wire figure', that is, all the edges may be seen) whose position in the ACTUAL coordinate system is equivalent to the following transformations on the SETUP figure with eight vertices $(\pm 1, \pm 1, \pm 1)$ given earlier

(1)   rotate the axes by an angle $\phi = 0.927295218$ radians about the z-axis. ($\cos \phi = 3/5$ and $\sin \phi = 4/5$);
(2)   move the origin to $(1, 0, 0)$;
(3)   rotate the axes by an angle $-\phi$ about the y-axis.

The ACTUAL triad is identified with the ABSOLUTE triad and the resulting projection is drawn in figure 6.2a. A plus sign is also drawn at the ABSOLUTE origin (using SYMBOL), to show its position and also the ABSOLUTE horizontal and vertical directions.

Matrix A, which effects the rotation of axes by the angle ϕ about the z-axis in the left-hand sense (which incidentally is the matrix necessary for rotating space through $-\phi$ about the same axis), is given by

$$A = \begin{pmatrix} \frac{3}{5} & \frac{4}{5} & 0 & 0 \\ \frac{-4}{5} & \frac{3}{5} & 0 & 0 \\ 0 & 0 & 1 & 0 \\ 0 & 0 & 0 & 1 \end{pmatrix} = \frac{1}{5} \begin{pmatrix} 3 & 4 & 0 & 0 \\ -4 & 3 & 0 & 0 \\ 0 & 0 & 5 & 0 \\ 0 & 0 & 0 & 5 \end{pmatrix}$$

Matrix B, which moves the origin to $(1, 0, 0)$, is

$$B = \begin{pmatrix} 1 & 0 & 0 & -1 \\ 0 & 1 & 0 & 0 \\ 0 & 0 & 1 & 0 \\ 0 & 0 & 0 & 1 \end{pmatrix}$$

Matrix C, which rotates the axes by $-\phi$ about the y-axis (equivalent to the matrix that rotates space by ϕ about the same axis), is

$$C = \frac{1}{5} \begin{pmatrix} 3 & 0 & 4 & 0 \\ 0 & 5 & 0 & 0 \\ -4 & 0 & 3 & 0 \\ 0 & 0 & 0 & 5 \end{pmatrix}$$

and the matrix that does the total transformation is $P = C \times B \times A$; remember that the order of the matrix multiplication is important!

$$P = \frac{1}{25} \begin{pmatrix} 9 & 12 & 20 & -15 \\ -20 & 15 & 0 & 0 \\ -12 & -16 & 15 & 20 \\ 0 & 0 & 0 & 25 \end{pmatrix}$$

The ACTUAL coordinates of the vertices of the cube are found by premultiplying the column-vector representation of each vertex in the SETUP system by P, and then changing the resulting column vector back into the standard three-dimensional form. Thus, the eight corners $(1, 1, 1)$, $(1, 1, -1)$, $(1, -1, 1)$, $(1, -1, -1)$, $(-1, 1, 1)$, $(-1, 1, -1)$, $(-1, -1, 1)$ and $(-1, -1, -1)$ are transformed to $(26/25, -1/5, 7/25)$, $(-14/25, -1/5, -23/25)$, $(2/25, -7/5, 39/25)$, $(-38/25, -7/5, 9/25)$, $(8/25, 7/5, 31/25)$, $(-32/25, 7/5, 1/25)$, $(-16/25, 1/5, 63/25)$ and $(-56/25, 1/5, 33/25)$, respectively. For example, $(1, 1, 1)$ transforms

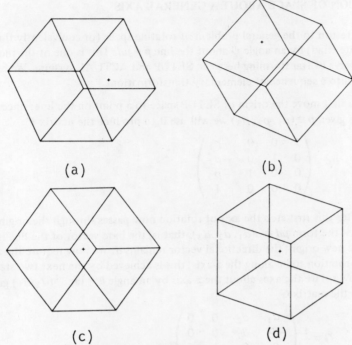

(a) (b)

(c) (d)

Figure 6.2

to $(26/25, -1/5, 7/25)$ because

$$\frac{1}{25}\begin{pmatrix} 9 & 12 & 20 & -15 \\ -20 & 15 & 0 & 0 \\ -12 & -16 & 15 & 20 \\ 0 & 0 & 0 & 25 \end{pmatrix} \times \begin{pmatrix} 1 \\ 1 \\ 1 \\ 1 \end{pmatrix} = \frac{1}{25}\begin{pmatrix} 26 \\ -5 \\ 7 \\ 25 \end{pmatrix}$$

To draw figure 6.2a, the projection of the 'wire cube', the z-coordinates of the above calculation are ignored, and the x and y-values are stored in the arrays XP and YP, and joined in pairs on the screen using the LINV array.

The ACTUAL subroutine to produce the matrix P for the above example is as follows.

```
      SUBROUTINE ACTUAL (P)
C ROUTINE TO CALCULATE THE ACTUAL MATRIX P.
      DIMENSION A(4,4),B(4,4),C(4,4),P(4,4),S(4,4)
      PHI=0.927295218
      CALL ROT(3,PHI,A)
      CALL TRAN(1.0,0.0,0.0,B)
      CALL ROT(2,-PHI,C)
      CALL MULT(B,A,S)
      CALL MULT(C,S,P)
      RETURN
      END
```

Program 6.7

ROTATION OF SPACE ABOUT A GENERAL AXIS

We now return to the general problem of rotating space (or equivalently the coordinate triad) by an angle ψ about the line $p + \mu d$. This is one of the most natural ways of transforming between SETUP and ACTUAL systems. We break the task into a sequence of elementary transformations.

(1)   We first move the origin of SETUP space to a point on the line; since we are given $p \equiv (p_1, p_2, p_3)$ we will use it to produce the matrix F

$$F = \begin{pmatrix} 1 & 0 & 0 & -p_1 \\ 0 & 1 & 0 & -p_2 \\ 0 & 0 & 1 & -p_3 \\ 0 & 0 & 0 & 1 \end{pmatrix}$$

After this first step the axis of rotation now passes through the origin and is of the form $\mu d \equiv \mu(d_1, d_2, d_3)$, that is, the base vector of the line is now the new origin; the directional vector remains d. We now require the axis of rotation to be along the z-axis; this is achieved by the next two steps.

(2)   Now rotate the axes about the z-axis by an angle $\theta = \tan^{-1}(d_2/d_1)$ given by the matrix G

$$G = \frac{1}{v} \begin{pmatrix} d_1 & d_2 & 0 & 0 \\ -d_2 & d_1 & 0 & 0 \\ 0 & 0 & v & 0 \\ 0 & 0 & 0 & v \end{pmatrix}$$

where the positive number v is given by $v^2 = d_1^2 + d_2^2$. Thus the point (d_1, d_2, d_3) transforms to $(v, 0, d_3)$, a point in the $x-z$ plane.

(3)   Then rotate the axes about the y-axis by an angle $\phi = \tan^{-1}(v/d_3)$ by the matrix H

$$H = \frac{1}{w} \begin{pmatrix} d_3 & 0 & -v & 0 \\ 0 & w & 0 & 0 \\ v & 0 & d_3 & 0 \\ 0 & 0 & 0 & w \end{pmatrix}$$

where the positive number w is given by $w^2 = v^2 + d_3^2 = d_1^2 + d_2^2 + d_3^2$. So the point $(v, 0, d_3)$ transforms into $(0, 0, w)$, a point on the z-axis. Since the origin transforms to an origin with both matrices G and H, the matrix combination $H \times G$ transforms any point on the line μd into a point on the z-axis in the new triad. Furthermore the combination $H \times G \times F$ transforms any point on the line $p + \mu d$ into a point on the new z-axis.

(4)   The problem of rotating space about a general axis has thus been reduced to rotating space about the z-axis. This is achieved by a matrix W, which rotates space by an angle ψ about the z-axis, that is, it rotates the triad of

axes by an angle $-\psi$ about the z-axis

$$W = \begin{pmatrix} \cos(-\psi) & \sin(-\psi) & 0 & 0 \\ -\sin(-\psi) & \cos(-\psi) & 0 & 0 \\ 0 & 0 & 1 & 0 \\ 0 & 0 & 0 & 1 \end{pmatrix} = \begin{pmatrix} \cos\psi & -\sin\psi & 0 & 0 \\ \sin\psi & \cos\psi & 0 & 0 \\ 0 & 0 & 1 & 0 \\ 0 & 0 & 0 & 1 \end{pmatrix}$$

(5) However, the required rotation is meant to be relative to the original axis positions. So we move the axes back by premultiplying by H^{-1}, G^{-1} and F^{-1} in order.

Thus the complete matrix sequence to solve the general rotation problem is given by $P = F^{-1} \times G^{-1} \times H^{-1} \times W \times H \times G \times F$. In essence, this is as though the ACTUAL triad is coincident with the SETUP triad although the space has been rotated about the general axis $p + \mu d$.

Naturally some of these matrices may reduce to the identity matrix and so be ignored. For example if the axis of rotation passes through the origin then both F and F^{-1} reduce to the identity matrix.

Example 6.2
Draw figure 6.2b, the cube defined by the SETUP routine in program 6.5, which has been rotated by -1 radian (in the left-hand sense) about the line $(0, 0, 1) + \mu(1, 1, 1)$.

The ACTUAL subroutine for producing matrix P is given below, and it is used in conjunction with the Main Program of program 6.6, together with all the other subroutines, MULT, etc.

```
      SUBROUTINE ACTUAL (P)
C ROUTINE TO CALCULATE THE ACTUAL MATRIX P NECESSARY TO ROTATE AN OBJECT
C ABOUT AN AXIS WITH DIRECTION (1,1,1) AND WHICH PASSES THROUGH (0,0,1).
      DIMENSION F(4,4),FM(4,4),G(4,4),GM(4,4),H(4,4),HM(4,4),W(4,4)
      DIMENSION A(4,4),B(4,4),P(4,4)
      CALL TRAN(0.0,0.0,1.0,F)
      CALL TRAN(0.0,0.0,-1.0,FM)
      CALL ANGLE(1.0,1.0,THETA)
      CALL ROT(3,THETA,G)
      CALL ROT(3,-THETA,GM)
      DD=SQRT(2.0)
      CALL ANGLE(1.0,DD,PHI)
      CALL ROT(2,PHI,H)
      CALL ROT(2,-PHI,HM)
      CALL ROT(3,1.0,W)
      CALL MULT(FM,GM,P)
      CALL MULT(HM,W,A)
      CALL MULT(P,A,B)
      CALL MULT(H,G,P)
      CALL MULT(P,F,A)
      CALL MULT(B,A,P)
      RETURN
      END
```

Program 6.8

THE GENERAL ORTHOGRAPHIC PROJECTION

The z-orthographic projection may be thought of as an observer placed at a
point on the negative z-axis, $(0, 0, -1)$, say, looking towards the origin.
ACTUAL space, that is, space relative to the ACTUAL coordinate system, is
then projected on to the plane whose normal is the line joining the observer to
the origin. A general orthographic projection is simply the case when the observer
is at some general point (EX, EY, EZ) in the ACTUAL system, and is looking
towards the origin, The projective plane now has this line as its normal.

This new projection is achieved by altering the axes once again, to produce an
OBSERVER triad whose origin is coincident with the ACTUAL origin and so
that the observer is on the negative z-axis of this new system. We then identify
the OBSERVER triad with the ABSOLUTE triad and create the z-orthographic
projection as usual.

To obtain the transformation between ACTUAL and OBSERVER systems,
we proceed in a manner similar to (2) and (3) in the last section.

(a)   produce a matrix D that changes the observer point from (EX, EY, EZ) to
      $(r, 0, EZ)$, where r is the positive solution to $r^2 = EX^2 + EY^2$, by rotating
      the axes about the axes by an angle $\theta = \tan^{-1}$ (EY/EX); thus the observer
      now lies in the x–z plane $(y = 0)$ of the latest triad

$$D = \frac{1}{r}\begin{pmatrix} EX & EY & 0 & 0 \\ -EY & EX & 0 & 0 \\ 0 & 0 & r & 0 \\ 0 & 0 & 0 & r \end{pmatrix}$$

(b)   then $(r, 0, EZ)$ is transformed by a matrix E to $(0, 0, -s)$ on the negative
      z-axis by rotating the axes by an angle $\phi + \pi$, $\phi = \tan^{-1}$ (r/EZ); s is the
      positive solution to $s^2 = r^2 + EZ^2 = EX^2 + EY^2 + EZ^2$

$$E = \frac{1}{s}\begin{pmatrix} -EZ & 0 & r & 0 \\ 0 & s & 0 & 0 \\ -r & 0 & -EZ & 0 \\ 0 & 0 & 0 & s \end{pmatrix}$$

We rotate by $\phi + \pi$ because by rotating by ϕ would put the observer on the
positive z-axis, and a z-orthographic projection would produce a mirror image of
the required projection.

Thus the matrix $Q = E \times D$ transforms the ACTUAL triad into the OBSERVER
triad, in any program the matrix Q is produced by a call to the OBSERVE
subroutine. This explains the entry in program 6.6 when it was used in example
6.1. It was assumed that the observer was already on the negative z-axis and thus
Q was the identity matrix.

The total transformation, that is, between SETUP and OBSERVER (=
ABSOLUTE) triads is achieved by the matrix $R = Q \times P$. Note it is the direction

of view that is important in the general orthographic projection, the precise position of the observer is not important. Thus the direction cosines of the line joining the origin to the observer (which has the opposite sense to the line of view) will be adequate to produce the ACTUAL-OBSERVER matrix Q.

Example 6.3
Produce figure 6.2c, the general orthographic projection of the ACTUAL space defined in example 6.1 when viewed from the point $(1/2, -1/2, 1/\sqrt{2})$.

$$D = \frac{1}{\sqrt{2}} \begin{pmatrix} 1 & -1 & 0 & 0 \\ 1 & 1 & 0 & 0 \\ 0 & 0 & \sqrt{2} & 0 \\ 0 & 0 & 0 & \sqrt{2} \end{pmatrix}$$

and

$$E = \frac{1}{\sqrt{2}} \begin{pmatrix} -1 & 0 & 1 & 0 \\ 0 & \sqrt{2} & 0 & 0 \\ -1 & 0 & -1 & 0 \\ 0 & 0 & 0 & \sqrt{2} \end{pmatrix}$$

and thus

$$Q = E \times D = \frac{1}{2} \begin{pmatrix} -1 & 1 & \sqrt{2} & 0 \\ \sqrt{2} & \sqrt{2} & 0 & 0 \\ -1 & 1 & -\sqrt{2} & 0 \\ 0 & 0 & 0 & 2 \end{pmatrix}$$

and the eight projected points (ignoring the z-coordinates) from the example become in order

$$\left(\frac{-31 + 7\sqrt{2}}{50}, \frac{21\sqrt{2}}{50} \right), \left(\frac{18 - 46\sqrt{2}}{50}, \frac{-19\sqrt{2}}{50} \right), \left(\frac{-37 + 39\sqrt{2}}{50}, \frac{-33\sqrt{2}}{50} \right),$$

$$\left(\frac{3 + 9\sqrt{2}}{50}, \frac{-73\sqrt{2}}{50} \right), \left(\frac{27 + 31\sqrt{2}}{50}, \frac{43\sqrt{2}}{50} \right), \left(\frac{67 + \sqrt{2}}{50}, \frac{3\sqrt{2}}{50} \right),$$

$$\left(\frac{21 + 63\sqrt{2}}{50}, \frac{-11\sqrt{2}}{50} \right), \left(\frac{61 + 33\sqrt{2}}{50}, \frac{-51\sqrt{2}}{50} \right)$$

In figure 6.2c, the origin, vertical and horizontal are implied by a plus sign.

A POSTSCRIPT TO THE GENERAL ORTHOGRAPHIC PROJECTION

When the OBSERVER triad was created, no mention was made regarding the positions of the x and y-axes; only the origin and the z-axis were considered. The x and y-directions in the OBSERVER space are those created by transforming the x and y-directions of ACTUAL space by Q. Further rotation of axes about the newly created z-axis will still leave the observer on the negative z-axis, and so orthographic projections after such further rotations will not change the shape of the projection; all that changes is the orientation. Which orientation do we choose? Are we satisfied with the axes produced by Q, or should we standardise the orientation in some way? One very popular standard form, which can be used provided the observer is not at a point on the ACTUAL y-axis, is one where a vertical (parallel to the y-axis) line in the ACTUAL system remains vertical in the OBSERVER system. This is known as 'maintaining the vertical', a form that will be used for the remainder of this book.

Since origin is transformed to origin by a rotation, we only need consider what happens to the point $(0, 1, 0)$ of the ACTUAL triad; if it is transformed into a point with zero x-coordinate then the vertical is maintained. After transforming by $Q = E \times D$, $(0, 1, 0)$ becomes $(Q(1, 2), Q(2, 2), Q(3, 2)) = (p, q, r)$, say. Note that since both E and D are rotations then $Q(1, 4) = Q(2, 4) = Q(3, 4) = 0$, and so they are not included in the values of p, q and r. If the axes are rotated about the z-axis through an angle $-\tan^{-1}(p/q)$ by a matrix V then the vertical is maintained

$$V = \frac{1}{t}\begin{pmatrix} q & -p & 0 & 0 \\ p & q & 0 & 0 \\ 0 & 0 & t & 0 \\ 0 & 0 & 0 & t \end{pmatrix}$$

where positive t satisfies $t^2 = p^2 + q^2$, and

$$V \times \begin{pmatrix} p \\ q \\ r \\ 1 \end{pmatrix} = \frac{1}{t}\begin{pmatrix} q & -p & 0 & 0 \\ p & q & 0 & 0 \\ 0 & 0 & t & 0 \\ 0 & 0 & 0 & t \end{pmatrix} \times \begin{pmatrix} p \\ q \\ r \\ 1 \end{pmatrix} = \begin{pmatrix} 0 \\ t \\ r \\ 1 \end{pmatrix}$$

which demonstrates the validity of this extra method. Hence we redefine the ACTUAL–OBSERVER matrix Q to be $Q = V \times E \times D$, and we incorporate these ideas in the OBSERVE subroutine.

```
      SUBROUTINE OBSERVE(Q)
C ROUTINE TO CALCULATE THE OBSERVATION MATRIX Q
C (THE VERTICAL IS MAINTAINED).
      DIMENSION Q(4,4),V(4,4),D(4,4),E(4,4),U(4,4)
      WRITE(6,1)
    1 FORMAT(* TYPE IN COORDINATES OF OBSERVATION POINT*)
      READ(5,*) EX,EY,EZ
      CALL ANGLE(EX,EY,THETA)
      CALL ROT(3,THETA,D)
      DD=SQRT(EX*EX+EY*EY)
      CALL ANGLE(EZ,DD,PHI)
      PHI=PHI+3.1415926535
      CALL ROT(2,PHI,E)
      CALL MULT(E,D,U)
      CALL ANGLE(U(2,2),U(1,2),PSI)
      CALL ROT(3,-PSI,V)
      CALL MULT(V,U,Q)
      RETURN
      END
```

Program 6.9

Example 6.4
Draw figure 6.2d, which is the same as figure 6.2c but with the vertical maintained.

This is achieved by a program containing the program segments of programs 6.6, 6.7 and 6.9, as well as the transformation routines, and subroutine ANGLE from chapter 2.

Exercise 6.1
It is essential to practise the techniques of this chapter, initially on simple geometrical solids (the Platonic solids — tetrahedra, etc. — and other symmetrical objects — cuboctahedra, etc.).

The choice of these objects has been kept simple so that the understanding of the transformation techniques is not confused by complexity in SETUP. The choice of transformations and observation points is endless, and they are left to the reader. To help practise we give the BLOCK DATA statements for a number of solids; the NOV and NOL in the subroutine SETUP must also be changed.

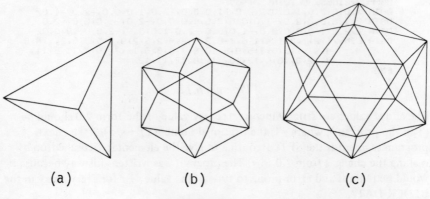

    (a)   (b)   (c)

Figure 6.3

Tetrahedron

In this case (figure 6.3a), NOV = 4 and NOL = 6.

```
      BLOCK DATA TETRA
C VERTEX AND LINE INFORMATION FOR A TETRAHEDRON.
      COMMON/VERTS/NOV,X(300),Y(300),Z(300),XP(300),YP(300)
      COMMON/LINES/NOL,LINV(2,400)
      DATA X/1.0,1.0,-1.0,-1.0/
      DATA Y/1.0,-1.0,1.0,-1.0/
      DATA Z/1.0,-1.0,-1.0,1.0/
      DATA LINV/1,2,1,3,1,4,2,3,2,4,3,4/
      END
```

Program 6.10

Cuboctahedron

In this case (figure 6.3b), NOV = 12 and NOL = 24.

```
      BLOCK DATA CUBOCT
C VERTEX AND LINE INFORMATION FOR A CUBOCTAHEDRON.
      COMMON/VERTS/NOV,X(300),Y(300),Z(300),XP(300),YP(300)
      COMMON/LINES/NOL,LINV(2,400)
      DATA X/0.0,1.0,1.0,0.0,1.0,-1.0,0.0,-1.0,1.0,0.0,-1.0,-1.0/
      DATA Y/1.0,0.0,1.0,-1.0,0.0,1.0,1.0,0.0,-1.0,-1.0,0.0,-1.0/
      DATA Z/1.0,1.0,0.0,1.0,-1.0,0.0,-1.0,1.0,0.0,-1.0,-1.0,0.0/
      DATA LINV/1,3,3,7,7,6,6,1,2,3,3,5,5,9,9,2,1,2,2,4,4,8,8,1,5,7,7,
     +         11,11,10,10,5,4,9,9,10,10,12,12,4,6,8,8,12,12,11,11,6/
      END
```

Program 6.11

Icosahedron

In this case (figure 6.3c) NOV = 12 and NOL = 30.

```
      BLOCK DATA ICOSA
C VERTEX AND LINE INFORMATION FOR AN ICOSAHEDRON.
      COMMON/VERTS/NOV,X(300),Y(300),Z(300),XP(300),YP(300)
      COMMON/LINES/NOL,LINV(2,400)
      DATA X/0.0,2.0,1.0,0.0,2.0,-1.0,0.0,-2.0,1.0,0.0,-2.0,-1.0/
      DATA Y/1.0,0.0,2.0,-1.0,0.0,2.0,1.0,0.0,-2.0,-1.0,0.0,-2.0/
      DATA Z/2.0,1.0,0.0,2.0,-1.0,0.0,-2.0,1.0,0.0,-2.0,-1.0,0.0/
      DATA LINV/1,2,1,3,1,4,1,6,1,8,2,3,2,4,2,5,2,9,3,5,3,6,3,7,4,8,
     +         4,9,4,12,5,7,5,9,5,10,6,7,6,8,6,11,7,10,7,11,8,11,
     +         8,12,9,10,9,12,10,11,10,12,11,12/
      END
```

Program 6.12

The above values are strictly incorrect; every value of the form 2.0 should be τ
(T in the program), where τ is the irrational number $(1 + \sqrt{5})/2$. The next
program segment is the SETUP routine to give the elementary icosahedron by
making the changes from 2.0 to τ. The program was written this way because it
would be tedious and error-prone to type in the value of τ for every entry in the
BLOCK DATA.

```
      SUBROUTINE SETUP
C SETUP AN ICOSAHEDRON.
      COMMON/VERTS/NOV,X(300),Y(300),Z(300),XP(300),YP(300)
      COMMON/LINES/NOL,LINV(2,400)
      NOV=12
      NOL=30
C REPLACE EVERY OCCURRENCE OF 2.0 IN THE DATA BY T.
      T=(1.0+SQRT(5.0))*0.5
      DO 1 I=1,NOV
      IF(ABS(X(I)).GT.1.5)X(I)=SIGN(T,X(I))
      IF(ABS(Y(I)).GT.1.5)Y(I)=SIGN(T,Y(I))
      IF(ABS(Z(I)).GT.1.5)Z(I)=SIGN(T,Z(I))
    1 CONTINUE
      RETURN
      END
```

Program 6.13

More complicated SETUPs will be discussed in chapter 9. Again note that the modular design of these routines means that SETUP, ACTUAL and OBSERVE can be changed independently to give a straightforward flexibility in the construction of diagrams.

Exercise 6.2
Produce the SETUP and BLOCK DATA statements for a pyramid, and incorporate them in a program to produce a variety of views of the object.

7 Perspective and Stereoscopic Views

We have seen how the orthographic projection is a valid and useful technique for displaying three-dimensional figures. However, it does not take into account the perspective phenomena of the real world: parallel lines appear to meet on the horizon; an object appears smaller as it recedes into the distance. Techniques for drawing such real situations have been devised by artists over the centuries, but these methods are of little value in computer graphics. Luckily the knowledge of three-dimensional coordinate geometry makes the drawing of objects in perspective relatively straightforward.

PERSPECTIVE VIEWS

To solve the problem we introduce a simplistic idea of what is meant by 'vision': specifically, that every visible point in space is seen because of a 'ray' coming from that point into the eye. Naturally the eye cannot see all of space; it is limited to a cone of rays that fall on the retina, the so-called 'cone of vision', which is outlined by the dashed lines in figure 7.1. To form a perspective view of space we place a 'perspective plane' perpendicular to the axis of the cone of vision — the 'straight-ahead' ray — and mark the points where each visible ray cuts this plane. This is quite a tall order, since there is an infinity of such points to consider. Actually the problem is not that great because we are dealing with points, lines and planes in three-dimensional space, and we shall see that we need only make a perspective projection of the important points, that is, the ends of line segments; of course, all plane segments are bounded by lines. The final view is formed by joining up pairs of projected points (if they are joined in three-dimensional space) or by labelling the points in some way.

Figure 7.1 shows a cube observed by an eye and projected on to two planes — the whole scene is also drawn in perspective! Two example rays are shown: the first is from the eye to A, one of the near corners of the cube, and the second to B, one of the far corners of the cube (far relative to the eye). The perspective projections of these points on to the near plane are A' and B', and on to the far plane A" and B". Note that the projections are the same shape and orientation, but they are of different sizes.

For simplicity in calculating the perspective projection of any object, we initially assume that the origin is the eye, and the 'straight-ahead ray' is the

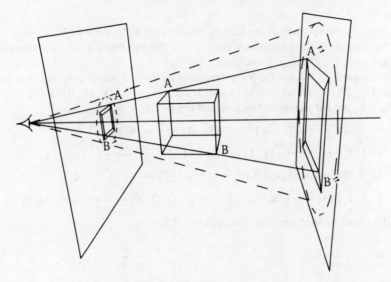

Figure 7.1

positive *z*-axis. If the perspective plane is a distance *d* (the variable PPD in later programs) from the eye, then we wish to calculate the coordinates in the $z = d$ plane of the points where the important rays cut the plane. In other words we wish to find the coordinates of $P' = (x', y', d)$, the projection point of $P = (x, y, z)$. Let us consider the *y*-coordinates by referring to figure 7.2. By similar triangles we see that $y'/d = y/z$, that is, $y' = y(d/z)$; and similarly, $x' = x(d/z)$ and hence $P' = (x(d/z), y(d/z), d)$. We can then identify the *x* and *y*-coordinates on the $z = d$ plane with the *x* and *y*-coordinates of the ABSOLUTE screen system, to produce the perspective view. The *z*-coordinate will be ignored because it is always equal to *d*.

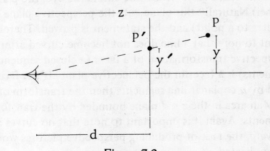

Figure 7.2

Example 7.1

Calculate the perspective projection of a cube with eight vertices $(0, 0, 4) +$ $(\pm 1, \pm 1, \pm 1)$ on to the perspective plane $z = 4$, the eye being at the origin and the 'straight-ahead ray' being the positive z-axis.

This space is in the simple form described in the last paragraph, and thus the point $(1, 1, 3)$ is transformed to $(1 \times 4/3, 1 \times 4/3, 4) = (1\frac{1}{3}, 1\frac{1}{3}, 4)$ and so in a similar way we get the eight transformed points

$$(1, 1, 3) \longrightarrow (1\tfrac{1}{3}, 1\tfrac{1}{3}); \qquad (1, -1, 3) \longrightarrow (1\tfrac{1}{3}, -1\tfrac{1}{3})$$

$$(-1, 1, 3) \longrightarrow (-1\tfrac{1}{3}, 1\tfrac{1}{3}); \qquad (-1, -1, 3) \longrightarrow (-1\tfrac{1}{3}, -1\tfrac{1}{3})$$

$$(1, 1, 5) \longrightarrow (4/5, 4/5); \qquad (1, -1, 5) \longrightarrow (4/5, -4/5)$$

$$(-1, 1, 5) \longrightarrow (-4/5, 4/5); \qquad (-1, -1, 5) \longrightarrow (-4/5, -4/5)$$

and the resulting diagram is shown in figure 7.3a.

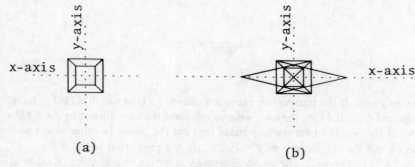

(a)   (b)

Figure 7.3

PROPERTIES OF A PERSPECTIVE TRANSFORMATION

(1)   The perspective transformation of a straight line is a straight line. This is implicitly obvious because the origin (the eye) and the line form a plane in three-dimensional space. (If the line enters the eye, the plane degenerates into a line.) Naturally this plane cuts the perspective plane in a line (or degenerates to a point) and the statement is proved. Therefore it is important to note that a line does not become curved after projection.

(2)   The perspective transformation of a facet (a closed sequence of coplanar line segments) is a facet in the perspective plane. If the facet is an area bounded by n coplanar line segments then the transform of this facet is naturally an area in the $z = d$ plane bounded by the transforms of the n line segments. Again it is important to note that no curves are introduced; if they were, the task of producing perspective pictures would be much more complicated.

(3) All infinitely long parallel lines appear to meet at one point — the vanishing point. If we take a general line from a set of parallel lines with direction vector h

$$p + \mu h \equiv (x_p, y_p, z_p) + \mu(x_h, y_h, z_h)$$

where $z_h > 0$, then the perspective transform of a general point on this line is

$$\left(\frac{(x_p + \mu x_h)d}{(z_p + \mu z_h)}, \frac{(y_p + \mu y_h)d}{(z_p + \mu z_h)} \right)$$

which can be rewritten as

$$\left(\frac{(x_h + x_p/\mu)d}{(z_h + z_p/\mu)}, \frac{(y_h + y_p/\mu)d}{(z_h + z_p/\mu)} \right)$$

As we move along the line towards large z-coordinates, that is, $\mu \to \infty$, then the line moves towards the vanishing point

$$\left(\frac{x_h d}{z_h}, \frac{y_h d}{z_h} \right)$$

This vanishing point is independent of p, the base point of the line, and hence all lines parallel to the direction h have the same vanishing point. Of course the case when $z_h < 0$ is ignored, because the line would disappear outside the cone of vision as $\mu \to \infty$.

(4) The vanishing points of all lines in parallel planes are collinear. Suppose that the set of parallel planes have a common normal direction $n \equiv (x_n, y_n, z_n)$. If a general line in one of these planes has direction h, then h is perpendicular to n (all lines in these planes are perpendicular to n). Thus $n \cdot h = 0$, that is, $x_n x_h + y_n y_h + z_n z_h = 0$, and dividing by z_h gives

$$x_n \frac{x_h}{z_h} + y_n \frac{y_h}{z_h} + z_n = 0$$

and so the vanishing point of these lines $(x_h d/z_h, y_h d/z_h)$ lies on the straight line $x_n x + y_n y + z_n d = 0$; and the statement is proved.

Example 7.2
Find the vanishing points of the edges of the cube in example 7.1, and of the diagonals of its top and bottom planes.

The twelve edges of the cube are divided into three sets of four edges; each set is parallel to the x, y and z-axis, respectively, and so the sets have directional vectors $(1, 0, 0)$, $(0, 1, 0)$ and $(0, 0, 1)$. The first two sets have zero z-values, and so their extended edges disappear outside the cone of vision, and are ignored. The third direction has vanishing point $(4 \times 0/1, 4 \times 0/1) = (0, 0)$ in two-dimensional space.

The diagonals have directions $(1, 0, 1)$, the major diagonal, and $(-1, 0, 1)$, the minor diagonal. The major diagonal on the top plane is $(-1, 1, 3) + \mu(1, 0, 1)$, and so the vanishing point is $(4 \times 1/1, 4 \times 0/1) = (4, 0)$. The minor diagonal on the top plane is $(1, 1, 3) + \mu(-1, 0, 1)$ and this vanishing point is $(4 \times -1/1, 4 \times 0/1) = (-4, 0)$. The vanishing points of the lines on the lower plane are also $(4, 0)$ and $(-4, 0)$. The relevant edges and diagonals are extended to their vanishing points to give figure 7.3b. Note that all the lines mentioned lie in the two parallel planes (the top and bottom of the cube), and so the vanishing points should be collinear; they are, because $(4, 0)$, $(0, 0)$ and $(-4, 0)$ all lie on the x-axis.

Exercise 7.1
Draw a perspective view of a tetrahedron, and also produce the vanishing points for some lines on the figure.

We now consider the program which draws perspective views. The first step is to produce the SETUP–ACTUAL–OBSERVER matrix R in the same way as with the orthographic projection program. The matrix R is used to transform each point in SETUP space into the OBSERVER space, but now these transformed values are used to overwrite the arrays X, Y and Z stored in /VERTS/. The eye (the observer) is placed at the point (EX, EY, EZ) of ACTUAL space (these values are read into the OBSERVE routine) and are transformed to the point $(0, 0, -\text{DIST})$ on the negative z-axis of OBSERVER space; $\text{DIST}^2 = \text{EX}^2 + \text{EY}^2 + \text{EZ}^2$. Unlike the orthographic projections, where only the direction of view mattered, the absolute position of the eye is essential when calculating a perspective view. If the perspective plane is a distance PPD from the eye, then we have all the information we need to do the calculations. In our theory the eye is the origin, but in OBSERVER space the eye is $(0, 0, -\text{DIST})$, so in the programs the value DIST must be added to every z-value in OBSERVER space in order to create the correct perspective view. Each point (XI, YI, ZI) relative to the OBSERVER triad is transformed to the point (XI*PPD/(ZI + DIST), YI*PPD/(ZI + DIST), PPD–DIST) on the perspective plane. We may ignore the z-value; the x and y-values are stored in the XP and YP arrays in /VERTS/. These points are joined, using the information in the LINV arrays exactly as we did in the orthographic projection. <u>The OBSERVE routine must be extended to calculate DIST and to store its value in Blank COMMON alongside PPD</u>. It must be noted that 'maintaining the vertical' now only refers to keeping the y axis of ACTUAL space vertical after transformation; lines parallel to this axis in ACTUAL and OBSERVER spaces need not be parallel after the perspective transformation.

```
C PROGRAM TO DRAW PERSPECTIVE PROJECTION OF A CUBE.
      COMMON/VERTS/NOV,X(300),Y(300),Z(300),XP(300),YP(300)
      COMMON/LINES/NOL,LINV(2,400)
      COMMON DIST,PPD
      DIMENSION P(4,4),Q(4,4),R(4,4)
```

```
C SETUP COORDINATES OF THE CUBE.
      CALL SETUP
C CALCULATE ACTUAL TRANSFORMATION MATRIX P AND THE OBSERVATION
C MATRIX Q, THEN FORM THEIR PRODUCT R.
      CALL ACTUAL(P)
      CALL OBSERVE(Q)
      CALL MULT(Q,P,R)
      WRITE(6,1)
    1 FORMAT(* TYPE IN DISTANCE OF EYE FROM PERSPECTIVE PLANE*)
      READ(5,*) PPD
C TRANSFORM THE CUBE COORDINATES USING MATRIX R.
      DO 2 I=1,NOV
      XI=R(1,1)*X(I)+R(1,2)*Y(I)+R(1,3)*Z(I)+R(1,4)
      YI=R(2,1)*X(I)+R(2,2)*Y(I)+R(2,3)*Z(I)+R(2,4)
      ZI=R(3,1)*X(I)+R(3,2)*Y(I)+R(3,3)*Z(I)+R(3,4)
      X(I)=XI
      Y(I)=YI
      Z(I)=ZI
C PERSPECTIVE TRANSFORM.
      DD=ZI+DIST
      XP(I)=XI*PPD/DD
      YP(I)=YI*PPD/DD
    2 CONTINUE
C NOW PLOT THE LINE SEGMENTS.
      CALL START(2)
      CALL PLOT(9.5,7.375,-3)
      DO 3 I=1,NOL
      I1=LINV(1,I)
      I2=LINV(2,I)
      CALL PLOT(XP(I1),YP(I1),3)
      CALL PLOT(XP(I2),YP(I2),2)
    3 CONTINUE
```

Program 7.1

Example 7.3

This program draws figure 7.4, the perspective view of a cube from the observer point (5, 10, 15), where the perspective plane is a distance of 33 (screen) inches from the eye. ACTUAL space is identical to the usual SETUP space for a cube. (Thus, the ACTUAL routine returns the identity matrix.) Naturally the same program will also draw the perspective view of any other object, or set of objects, provided their data description fits into the COMMON stores, /VERTS/, etc.

The image shown in figure 7.4 was produced on microfilm, which was then used as a photographic negative; naturally the size of the picture depends on the

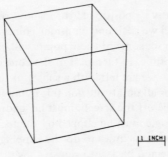

|1 INCH|

Figure 7.4

printing of the film. Hence a line with a length of 1 screen inch is drawn in this, and most of the following perspective views, to show the correct scale of the picture. So as to get a correct view of figure 7.4, it should be viewed at a distance of 33 times this screen inch, that is about 9 (true) inches.

Exercise 7.2
Practise using this technique on tetrahedra, cuboctahedra, etc.

THE CHOICE OF PERSPECTIVE PLANE

Once the position of the eye relative to the object (or space) is fixed, then the shape of the perspective image of the object is independent of the placing of the perspective plane (see figure 7.1). All that changes with the position of the plane (that is, the value of PPD) is the size of the image. So which perspective plane do we choose? If a series of pictures is to be produced, then for consistency we naturally keep the same perspective plane, but what is the value of PPD?

Of course we have to consider the practical situation: namely, there is a person (the observer) sitting in front of a graphics console and *one* (?) of his eyes is looking towards the screen origin and is focused on the screen surface. (Note that with perspective projections the whole of space seems to be in focus.) The natural perspective plane distance is the distance of the eye from the screen, measured in screen inches. With this choice of PPD the eye gets a 'true' view of the coordinate space. This distance is usually 4 times the half-depth of the screen (that is, PPD is approximately equal to $4 \times 8.25 = 33$ screen inches). If the perspective plane is placed between the eye and the screen we get a smaller image, which is then perpendicularly transmitted back on to the screen. If the plane is beyond the screen then the image appears to be magnified, and we get a 'close-up' effect. See also project 17, p. 137.

CLIPPING

Theoretically, objects may be positioned throughout observer space, even behind the eye, although we shall only consider points with z-value positive in respect to the eye. Even so, some of these points will be outside the cone of vision and therefore invisible. In fact, part of the cone of vision will still be outside the screen area — we are left with a subset of the cone of vision, the 'pyramid of vision'. Thus all points outside this pyramid, that is, those whose perspective transforms lie off the screen, must be ignored, and line segments outside the screen rectangle must be clipped by the techniques of chapter 4. Most 'scopes have hardware facilities to do the clipping; however, some microfilm users may find lines reflected back into view if they do not clip the diagrams.

STEREOSCOPIC VIEWS

Perspective projections are all very well but unfortunately (or fortunately!) we have two eyes. Each eye should have its own perspective view, which will differ slightly from that of the other eye. This is the means by which we appreciate the three-dimensional quality of our world. And this is exactly what we shall do to produce a stereoscopic view of space, namely, calculate a perspective view for each eye. This leads to a problem: we cannot simply draw two such projections, because the left eye will not only see the view created for it, but also that made for the right eye. To stop this confusion, we must ensure that each eye sees its own view, but only its view. There are two methods available: the stereoscope, and filters. The stereoscope is a device that creates a form of tunnel vision, ensuring a narrow cone of vision for each eye. The computer must produce a hard copy that will fit into the stereoscope so that the two images are seen, one in each cone of vision. Naturally the images must not overlap, and so the images are necessarily small — a major drawback with the instrument. The other method, the filter, is a pair of transparent plastics sheets, one red (left eye) and one green (right eye). In this way the left eye cannot see red lines and the green lines appear black; the reverse is true for the right eye. So the computer must make a hard copy of two images, one in green for the left eye and the other in red for the right eye. The brain then merges the two images to give a three-dimensional effect.

So we wish to devise a method of producing the stereoscopic transformation of a general point $P = (x, y, z)$, that is, the two points $PL = (x_1, y_1)$ for the left eye and $PR = (x_r, y_r)$ for the right, in the coordinate system of the perspective plane. (We sensibly use the same perspective plane for both eyes.) In order to describe the method, we simplify the coordinate system of space: we assume that the origin is between the eyes and the direction of view for each eye

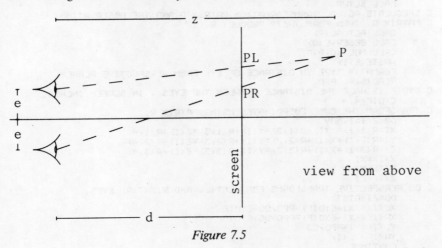

Figure 7.5

(straight ahead) is parallel to the z-axis. The eyes have coordinates $(-e, 0, 0)$, left, and $(e, 0, 0)$, right; in the program e is the variable EYDIF and the arrays holding the stereo points are (XL, YL) and (XR, YR); see figure 7.5. Again the perspective plane is a distance d from the origin. In order to find PL, we change the origin to $(-e, 0, 0)$ and so P becomes $(x + e, y, z)$ and the perspective transform of this point for the left eye is $((x + e)d/z, yd/z)$, which, when the coordinate axes are returned to their original position, becomes $((x + e)d/z - e, yd/z)$. Similarly, the right-eye transformation produces PR = $((x - e)d/z + e, yd/z)$. The program to produce the stereoscopic picture of space is very similar to the perspective program, except that, instead of storing values in the XP and YP arrays, the two sets of values are placed in the arrays XL, YL, XR, YR.

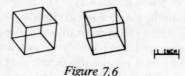

Figure 7.6

Example 7.4
Draw figure 7.6, a stereoscopic view of a cube, SETUP as in previous examples and in an ACTUAL space identified with the SETUP space. The eyes are 8.8 screen inches apart (EYDIF = 4.4); the observer point is (10, 20, 30); and the perspective plane is a distance of 25 screen inches from the eye.

```
C PROGRAM TO DRAW STEREOSCOPIC VIEW OF A CUBE.
      COMMON/VERTS/NOV,X(300),Y(300),Z(300),XL(300),YL(300),XR(300),YR(3
     +00)
      COMMON/LINES/NOL,LINV(2,400)
      COMMON DIST,PPD
      DIMENSION P(4,4),Q(4,4),R(4,4)
C SETUP COORDINATES OF THE CUBE.
      CALL SETUP
C CALCULATE ACTUAL TRANSFORMATION MATRIX P AND THE OBSERVATION
C MATRIX Q, THEN FORM THEIR PRODUCT R.
      CALL ACTUAL(P)
      CALL OBSERVE(Q)
      CALL MULT(Q,P,R)
      WRITE(6,1)
    1 FORMAT(* TYPE IN DISTANCE OF EYE FROM PERSPECTIVE PLANE*)
      READ(5,*) PPD
C EYDIF IS HALF THE DISTANCE BETWEEN THE EYES , IN SCREEN INCHES.
      EYDIF=4.4
C TRANSFORM THE CUBE COORDINATES USING MATRIX R.
      DO 2 I=1,NOV
      XI=R(1,1)*X(I)+R(1,2)*Y(I)+R(1,3)*Z(I)+R(1,4)
      YI=R(2,1)*X(I)+R(2,2)*Y(I)+R(2,3)*Z(I)+R(2,4)
      ZI=R(3,1)*X(I)+R(3,2)*Y(I)+R(3,3)*Z(I)+R(3,4)
      X(I)=XI
      Y(I)=YI
      Z(I)=ZI
C DO PERSPECTIVE TRANSFORMS FOR LEFT(L) AND RIGHT(R) EYES.
      DD=ZI+DIST
      XL(I)=(XI+EYDIF)*PPD/DD-EYDIF
      XR(I)=(XI-EYDIF)*PPD/DD+EYDIF
      YL(I)=YI*PPD/DD
      YR(I)=YL(I)
    2 CONTINUE
```

```
C NOW PLOT THE LINE SEGMENTS.
      CALL START(2)
      CALL PLOT(9.5,7.375,-3)
C DRAW LEFT EYE DIAGRAM.
      DO 3 I=1,NOL
      I1=LINV(1,I)
      I2=LINV(2,I)
      CALL PLOT(XL(I1),YL(I1),3)
      CALL PLOT(XL(I2),YL(I2),2)
    3 CONTINUE
C DRAW RIGHT EYE DIAGRAM.
      DO 4 I=1,NOL
      I1=LINV(1,I)
      I2=LINV(2,I)
      CALL PLOT(XR(I1),YR(I1),3)
      CALL PLOT(XR(I2),YR(I2),2)
    4 CONTINUE
```

Program 7.2

Even without a stereoscope or filters, it is still possible to appreciate the three-dimensional effect of this figure by placing a card vertically between the two cubes and concentrating each eye, one on either side of the card. The scene should be viewed at a distance of 25 screen inches, that is, just over 6 in.

Exercise 7.3
Practise these techniques on icosahedra and cuboctahedra.

8 Hidden Line Algorithms

All the three-dimensional diagrams drawn so far have been 'wire figures', pictures of objects in which all edges and vertices may be seen. If an object is solid, then naturally the edges and vertices behind the volume of the object would be invisible to an observer, for example, the dashed lines in figure 8.1. So we have to produce a Hidden Line Algorithm that will draw only the visible line segments on a solid object or set of objects. We shall assume that all vertices are the end points of line segments.

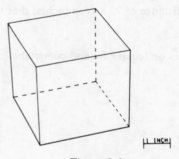

Figure 8.1

There are a number of such algorithms — some simple, some very sophisticated. Some only work on special, peculiarly defined objects, whereas others work on all combinations of objects. These general algorithms are therefore more complicated; however, they may be limited by time and storage restrictions. We will give two methods to be used in conjunction with a perspective transformation: the first is of the simple type, while the second is a slightly restricted form of a general Hidden Line Algorithm.

Before we can deal with these algorithms it is necessary to consider what additional information is required regarding objects in SETUP space. So far, we only store vertex and line information; Hidden Line Algorithms check whether lines lie behind plane segments (or facets) on the surface of the solid objects. This required facet information is placed in the COMMON block /FACETS/ and consists of NOF, the number of facets on the objects in space, and the arrays INDEXF and LINF. Here LINF(I, J) is the index of the Ith line that bounds the Jth facet, there being INDEXF(J) such lines defining the Jth facet. The line segments are assumed to be in a clockwise (or anticlockwise) order around the facet, which in turn is assumed to be convex. We allow for 200 facets and a maximum of six lines bounding each.

COMMON /FACETS/ NOF, INDEXF(200), LINF(6, 200)

If in any diagram non-convex facets appear, or a facet is bounded by more than six edges, then they may be subdivided into subfacets of the correct form. For the cube used in the last two chapters, NOF = 6 must be added to the SETUP routine and the BLOCK DATA routine now takes the following form.

```
BLOCK DATA BLOCKS
COMMON/VERTS/NOV,X(300),Y(300),Z(300),XP(300),YP(300)
COMMON/LINES/NOL,LINV(2,400)
COMMON/FACETS/NOF,INDEXF(200),LINF(6,200)
DATA X/1.0,1.0,1.0,1.0,-1.0,-1.0,-1.0,-1.0/
DATA Y/1.0,1.0,-1.0,-1.0,1.0,1.0,-1.0,-1.0/
DATA Z/1.0,-1.0,1.0,-1.0,1.0,-1.0,1.0,-1.0/
DATA LINV/1,2,2,4,4,3,3,1,5,6,6,8,8,7,7,5,1,5,2,6,4,8,3,7/
DATA INDEXF/4,4,4,4,4,4,4,4,4,4,4,4/
DATA LINF/1,2,3,4,0,0,5,6,7,8,0,0,1,10,5,9,0,0,
+         2,11,6,10,0,0,3,11,7,12,0,0,4,12,8,9,0,0/
END
```

Program 8.1

In the algorithms that follow we assume that the SETUP–ACTUAL–OBSERVER matrix R has been calculated and each point of SETUP space (the X, Y and Z arrays) is transformed to its position in OBSERVER space by R. We differ from our earlier programs by now overwriting these X, Y and Z arrays with the corresponding coordinates of the transformed points. The perspective projection of each point is calculated and stored in the XP and YP arrays (as in chapter 7).

AN ALGORITHM FOR THREE-DIMENSIONAL CONVEX BODIES CONTAINING THE ORIGIN

The algorithm we give first is elementary, and can only be used on single convex bodies; a convex body in three dimensions is one where a line joining any two points in the body lies totally inside the body. The method also requires that the origin of OBSERVER space lie inside the body. Because of this restriction, we know that any facet may be seen if and only if the infinite plane containing the facet cuts the line joining the eye $(0, 0, -DIST)$ to the origin between these two points. That is, the plane in OBSERVER space cuts the z-axis at a point between $(0, 0, -DIST)$ and $(0, 0, 0)$. If it cuts beyond the origin — that is, the positive z-axis or behind the eye at $(0, 0, z)$, where $z < -DIST$, then if the object were transparent we would see the underside of the facet. In this case all points on the facet, except possibly those on the edges of the facet, would be hidden. The edges may be seen because they may also be in another visible facet.

In order to discover whether the Jth facet is visible or not, we take three points $\{(x_i, y_i, z_i) \mid i = 1, 2, 3\}$ from the facet. Suppose that $I1 = LINF(1, J)$ and $I2 = LINF(2, J)$ are the indices of two lines in the facet; then the four vertex indices $LINV(1, I1)$, $LINV(2, I1)$, $LINV(1, I2)$ and $LINV(2, I2)$ will contain the indices of three non-collinear points, as required. Using the techniques of chapter 5, in particular example 5.4, we can use these three vertices to calculate the equation of the plane containing the facet, $ax + by + cz = d$. Putting this equation in functional form, $f(x, y, z) \equiv ax + by + cz - d$, we can discover if the origin $(0, 0, 0)$ and observer $(0, 0, -DIST)$ lie on the same side of the plane by comparing the sign of $f(0, 0, 0)$, that is, the sign of $-d$, with the sign of $f(0, 0, -DIST)$, that is, the sign of $-d - c \times DIST$. Hence the facet is visible if and only if $d + c \times DIST$ is of opposite sign to d. This calculation can be made for each facet; if the facet is visible, the indices of all its boundary edges are added to an array LIST. Naturally, a line that is the boundary between two visible facets will appear twice in LIST. By putting the array into increasing numerical order and then deleting duplications, we are left with the indices of all the visible lines in the object. Using this information, and that stored in LINV, all these lines may be drawn to complete a hidden-line perspective picture.

Example 8.1
Produce the hidden line picture in figure 8.1 of the cube shown in figure 7.4.

With this simple case, lines are either totally visible or totally invisible. Thus a line with an index not in LIST is invisible. In the program to solve this exercise an extra facility is added — if it is required to illustrate the overall shape of the figure, the hidden lines may be 'shown' as dashed lines. The dashes must be shown in perspective: for the figure to make sense the dashes must appear smaller as they recede from the eye.

```
C PROGRAM TO DRAW PERSPECTIVE PROJECTION OF A CONVEX OBJECT
C USING A HIDDEN LINE ALGORITHM.
      COMMON/VERTS/NOV,X(300),Y(300),Z(300),XP(300),YP(300)
      COMMON/LINES/NOL,LINV(2,400)
      COMMON/FACETS/NOF,INDEXF(200),LINF(6,200)
      COMMON DIST,PPD
      DIMENSION P(4,4),Q(4,4),R(4,4)
C SETUP COORDINATES OF THE OBJECT.
      CALL SETUP
C CALCULATE ACTUAL TRANSFORMATION MATRIX P AND THE OBSERVATION
C MATRIX Q, THEN FORM THEIR PRODUCT R.
      CALL ACTUAL(P)
      CALL OBSERVE(Q)
      CALL MULT(Q,P,R)
      WRITE(6,1)
    1 FORMAT(* TYPE IN DISTANCE OF EYE FROM PERSPECTIVE PLANE*)
      READ(5,*) PPD
C TRANSFORM THE OBJECT COORDINATES USING MATRIX R.
      DO 2 I=1,NOV
      XI=R(1,1)*X(I)+R(1,2)*Y(I)+R(1,3)*Z(I)+R(1,4)
      YI=R(2,1)*X(I)+R(2,2)*Y(I)+R(2,3)*Z(I)+R(2,4)
      ZI=R(3,1)*X(I)+R(3,2)*Y(I)+R(3,3)*Z(I)+R(3,4)
      X(I)=XI
      Y(I)=YI
      Z(I)=ZI
      DD=ZI+DIST
```

```
      XP(I)=XI*PPD/DD
      YP(I)=YI*PPD/DD
    2 CONTINUE
      CALL START(2)
      CALL PLOT(9.5,7.375,-3)
      CALL HIDDEN
      CALL ENPLOT
      STOP
      END
```

Program 8.2

```
      SUBROUTINE HIDDEN
C SIMPLE HIDDEN LINE ALGORITHM FOR USE WITH CONVEX BODIES
C CONTAINING THE ORIGIN.
      DIMENSION LIST(200)
      COMMON/VERTS/NOV,X(300),Y(300),Z(300),XP(300),YP(300)
      COMMON/LINES/NOL,LINV(2,400)
      COMMON/FACETS/NOF,INDEXF(200),LINF(6,200)
      COMMON DIST,PPD
      IHID=0
      IC=0
C LIST(I) I=1..IC WILL CONTAIN THE INDICES OF THE LINES WHICH ARE
C ON PLANES WHICH CUT THE LINE BETWEEN THE ORIGIN AND EYE.
      DO 3 I=1,NOF
      I1=LINF(1,I)
      I2=LINF(2,I)
C FROM FIRST TWO LINES IN I'TH PLANE FIND IV1,IV2 AND IV3 ,
C THE INDICES OF THREE DIFFERENT POINTS IN THE PLANE.
      IV1=LINV(1,I1)
      IV2=LINV(2,I1)
      IV3=LINV(1,I2)
      IF(IV1.EQ.IV3.OR.IV2.EQ.IV3) IV3=LINV(2,I2)
C CALCULATE THE PLANE A.X + B.Y + C.Z = D CONTAINING THESE POINTS.
      DX1=X(IV1)-X(IV2)
      DY1=Y(IV1)-Y(IV2)
      DZ1=Z(IV1)-Z(IV2)
      DX3=X(IV3)-X(IV2)
      DY3=Y(IV3)-Y(IV2)
      DZ3=Z(IV3)-Z(IV2)
      A=DY1*DZ3-DY3*DZ1
      B=DZ1*DX3-DZ3*DX1
      C=DX1*DY3-DX3*DY1
C (X(IV1),Y(IV1),Z(IV1)) LIES IN THIS PLANE THUS ....
      D=A*X(IV1)+B*Y(IV1)+C*Z(IV1)
C (0.0,0.0,0.0) AND (0.0,0.0,-DIST) LIE ON OPPOSITE SIDES OF THE
C PLANE IF F IS LESS THAN 0.0 .
      F=1.0+C*DIST/D
      IF(F.GE.0.0) GO TO 3
C PUT THE INDEX OF EVERY LINE IN THE I'TH PLANE INTO ARRAY LIST.
C THIS WILL NATURALLY LEAD TO DUPLICATION OF LINE INDICES IN ARRAY.
      IXX=INDEXF(I)
      DO 2 J=1,IXX
      IC=IC+1
      LIST(IC)=LINF(J,I)
    2 CONTINUE
    3 CONTINUE
C PUT ARRAY LIST INTO INCREASING NUMERICAL ORDER.
      IC1=IC-1
      DO 5 I=1,IC1
      II=I+1
      LL=LIST(I)
      DO 4 J=II,IC
      IF(LL.LE.LIST(J)) GO TO 4
      LL=LIST(J)
      LIST(J)=LIST(I)
      LIST(I)=LL
    4 CONTINUE
    5 CONTINUE
```

```
C NOW GET RID OF DUPLICATIONS IN THE ARRAY LIST.
      J=1
      DO 6 I=2,IC
      IF(LIST(I).EQ.LIST(J)) GO TO 6
      J=J+1
      LIST(J)=LIST(I)
    6 CONTINUE
      IC=J
      INL=1
      LINEQ=LIST(1)
C FOR EACH LINE IN THE FIGURE DO -
C IF LINE INDEX IS IN ARRAY LIST THEN DRAW LINE
C ELSE IF IHID=1 THEN DRAW DASHED LINE
C      ELSE IGNORE THE LINE.
      DO 8 I=1,NOL
      L2=LINV(2,I)
      L1=LINV(1,I)
      IF(I.NE.LINEQ.OR.INL.GT.IC) GO TO 7
      CALL PLOT(XP(L1),YP(L1),3)
      CALL PLOT(XP(L2),YP(L2),2)
      INL=INL+1
      LINEQ=LIST(INL)
      GO TO 8
    7 IF(IHID.NE.1) GO TO 8
      CALL DASH(L1,L2)
    8 CONTINUE
      RETURN
      END
```

Program 8.3

```
      SUBROUTINE DASH(L1,L2)
C SUBROUTINE TO DRAW A DASHED LINE ( IN PERSPECTIVE ) BETWEEN
C THE PERSPECTIVE POINTS WITH INDICES L1 AND L2.
      COMMON/VERTS/NOV,X(200),Y(200),Z(200),XP(200),YP(200)
      COMMON/LINES/NOL,LINV(2,200)
      COMMON/FACETS/NOF,INDEXF(200),LINF(6,200)
      COMMON DIST,PPD
C THE END POINTS OF THE LINE IN 3-D SPACE ARE (X1,Y1,Z1) AND (X2,Y2,
      X1=X(L1)
      Y1=Y(L1)
      Z1=Z(L1)
      X2=X(L2)
      Y2=Y(L2)
      Z2=Z(L2)
C THERE WILL BE (M/2)+1 DASHES, EACH APPROXIMATELY 0.1 INCHES LONG,
C 3-D SPACE. THESE WILL BE THEN TRANSFORMED INTO PERPSECTIVE SPACE.
      DD=SQRT((X1-X2)**2+(Y1-Y2)**2+(Z1-Z2)**2)
      M=IFIX(DD*10.0)
      IF(MOD(M,2).EQ.0)M=M+1
      R=FLOAT(M)
      M1=M-1
      XBIT=(X2-X1)/R
      YBIT=(Y2-Y1)/R
      ZBIT=(Z2-Z1)/R
      RX=XP(L1)
      RY=YP(L1)
      CALL PLOT(RX,RY,3)
      MODE=3
C MOVE (X1,Y1,Z1) ALONG THE LINE - ALTERNATING MODES BETWEEN 2 AND 3
C THUS PRODUCING THE DASHED LINE.
      DO 1 J=1,M1
      MODE=5-MODE
      X1=X1+XBIT
      Y1=Y1+YBIT
      Z1=Z1+ZBIT
      RZ=PPD/(DIST+Z1)
```

```
C CALCULATE THE PERSPECTIVE TRANSFORM OF (X1,Y1,Z1) - I.E. (RX,RY)
C AND THEN MOVE THE PLOT HEAD TO THIS POINT IN THE PRESENT MODE.
      RX=X1*RZ
      RY=Y1*RZ
      CALL PLOT(RX,RY,MODE)
    1 CONTINUE
      CALL PLOT(XP(L2),YP(L2),2)
      RETURN
      END
```

Program 8.4

Exercise 8.1

Produce the program for an orthographic Hidden Line Algorithm for use with a convex body containing the origin.

Now the observer point has no positional meaning: it only gives the normal to the orthographic plane, and is the means of producing the ACTUAL–OBSERVER matrix. In this case, a facet is seen if and only if the infinite plane containing it cuts the negative z-axis. If the plane is given by the function $f(x, y, z) \equiv ax + by + cz - d$, then it cuts the z-axis at $(0, 0, z')$, where $f(0, 0, z') = cz' - d = 0$, that is, $z' = d/c$. Thus the necessary and sufficient condition for a facet in the plane $f(x, y, z) = 0$ to be seen is that c and d must have opposite signs.

Exercise 8.2

Produce a stereoscopic Hidden Line Algorithm for a convex body containing the origin.

A GENERAL HIDDEN LINE ALGORITHM

There is a restriction to the use of the algorithm that follows (another subroutine called HIDDEN): namely, no pair of facets intersect on a line that is not given in the LINV array. Again the objects are defined in SETUP space and the vertices transformed by the matrix R to arrays X, Y and Z; the perspective transformations of these vertices are also placed in the XP and YP arrays.

In order to produce a hidden line picture of OBSERVER space, each line on the objects must be compared with every facet; now, of course, parts of a line may be visible and parts invisible (behind a facet). We suppose that a typical line Γ_3 in OBSERVER space joins the two points (x_1', y_1', z_1') and (x_2', y_2', z_2'); thus a general point on this line is

$$(1 - \phi)(x_1', y_1', z_1') + \phi(x_2', y_2', z_2')$$

And we suppose that these two points are perspectively projected on to the two points (x_1, y_1) and (x_2, y_2) on the perspective plane. Thus Γ_3 is projected to the line Γ_2 in this plane with the general point

$$(1 - \lambda)(x_1, y_1) + \lambda(x_2, y_2)$$

Note The point $(1 - \phi)(x'_1, y'_1, z'_1) + \phi(x'_2, y'_2, z'_2)$ does not transform into $(1 - \phi)(x_1, y_1) + \phi(x_2, y_2)$, that is, ϕ is not necessarily equal to λ.

We let a typical facet Ω_3 be projected to an area Ω_2 on the perspective plane, and we assume that the vertices on this projected facet are

$$\nabla = \{(\bar{x}_i, \bar{y}_i) \mid i = 1, \ldots, \text{IN}\}$$

Thus the ith edge in Ω_2 has a general point $(1 - \mu)(\bar{x}_i, \bar{y}_i) + \mu(\bar{x}_{i+1}, \bar{y}_{i+1})$ where $0 \leqslant \mu \leqslant 1$. Again, the addition of subscripts is modulo IN.

In an ordinary perspective picture every line Γ_2 would be drawn on the screen; now, however, if a facet Ω_3 lies between the eye and Γ_3 then part, and perhaps all, of Γ_2 will be hidden. Most facets do not interfere with the view of any one line, and so we sift out some of the easily recognisable possibilities.

If Γ_3 lies in the facet Ω_3, then Γ_3 is on the surface of the facet and any view of this line cannot be obscured by that facet. This is easily checked by comparing the line index of Γ_3 with the indices of the edges of the facet. If the line is not an edge of the facet then it has to be considered in detail.

If Ω_2 is not intersected by Γ_2, then Ω_3 can have no effect on the line. There are three elementary possibilities given

(1)   the vertices ∇ all lie on the same side of Γ_2;
(2) ∇ all lie on the opposite side of (x_1, y_1) to (x_2, y_2);
(3) ∇ all lie on the opposite side of (x_2, y_2) to (x_1, y_1).

We check them individually.

(1) $f(x, y) = (y - y_1)(x_2 - x_1) - (x - x_1)(y_2 - y_1)$ is the functional representation of Γ_2. If $f(\bar{x}_i, \bar{y}_i)$ has the same sign for all vertices $(\bar{x}_i, \bar{y}_i)$ belonging to ∇, then all the vertices of Ω_2 lie on the same side of Γ_2 and there is no intersection between Γ_2 and Ω_2.

(2) $g(x, y) = (y - y_1)(y_2 - y_1) + (x - x_1)(x_2 - x_1)$ is the functional representation of the line through (x_1, y_1) perpendicular to Γ_2. If the sign of $g(x_2, y_2)$ is not equal to the sign of $g(\bar{x}_i, \bar{y}_i)$ for all $(\bar{x}_i, \bar{y}_i)$ belonging to ∇, then Γ_2 does not intersect Ω_2.

(3) $h(x, y) = (y - y_2)(y_2 - y_1) + (x - x_2)(x_2 - x_1)$ is the line through (x_2, y_2) perpendicular to Γ_2. In a manner similar to (2), a facet is ignored if the sign of $h(x_1, y_1)$ is not equal to the sign of $h(\bar{x}_i, \bar{y}_i)$ for all $(\bar{x}_i, \bar{y}_i)$.

Any facet that passes this first hurdle has to be considered in detail. We assume that Γ_2 cuts the extended ith edge of Ω_2 at the point

$$(1 - \mu_i)(\bar{x}_i, \bar{y}_i) + \mu_i(\bar{x}_{i+1}, \bar{y}_{i+1})$$

If $\mu_i < 0$ or $\mu_i > 1$ then Γ_2 intersects the ith edge at a point outside the area Ω_2; if $0 \leqslant \mu_i \leqslant 1$ then Γ_2 crosses the area Ω_2 at a point on its ith edge. Since the perspective projection of a convex facet is a convex area on the perspective plane (the reader should prove this), then the number of crossing points is either zero (and hence there is no intersection, and the facet is ignored) or two. In this latter case we find the two crossing points on the line Γ_2 given by the values μ_{min} and $\mu_{max}, \mu_{min} < \mu_{max}$, that is the points are $(1 - \mu_{min})(x_1, y_1) + \mu_{min}(x_2, y_2)$ and $(1 - \mu_{max})(x_1, y_1) + \mu_{max}(x_2, y_2)$.

It is now necessary to discover whether the subsegment of Γ_2 between these two points is visible or not. This is checked by finding the mid-point of the segment $(x_{mid}, y_{mid}) = (1 - \mu_{mid})(x_1, y_1) + \mu_{mid}(x_2, y_2)$, where $\mu_{mid} = (\mu_{max} + \mu_{min})/2$. We then find the point $(\hat{x}, \hat{y}, \hat{z})$ on Γ_3 that has (x_{mid}, y_{mid}) as its perspective projection. The line segment is hidden if and only if $(\hat{x}, \hat{y}, \hat{z})$ and the eye lie on opposite sides of the infinite plane containing Ω_3. The equation of this plane is found using the technique given in the simple Hidden Line Algorithm, and its functional representation can be used to check the above requirement. *Note* $\hat{x} \times PPD/(\hat{z} + DIST) = \hat{x}_{mid}$ and $\hat{y} \times PPD/(\hat{z} + DIST) = \hat{y}_{mid}$ and $(\hat{x}, \hat{y}, \hat{z})$ lies on Γ_3, so for some value of ϕ, $\hat{x} = (1 - \phi)x'_1 + \phi x'_2$; $\hat{y} = (1 - \phi)y'_1 + \phi y'_2$; $\hat{z} = (1 - \phi)z'_1 + \phi z'_2$. Hence

$$x_{mid} = \frac{(x'_1 + \phi(x'_2 - x'_1))PPD}{z'_1 + \phi(z'_2 - z'_1) + DIST}$$

and

$$y_{mid} = \frac{(y'_1 + \phi(y'_2 - y'_1))PPD}{z'_1 + \phi(z'_2 - z'_1) + DIST}$$

that is

$$\phi = \frac{x_{mid}(z'_1 + DIST) - x'_1 PPD}{(x'_2 - x'_1)PPD - x_{mid}(z'_2 - z'_1)} = \frac{y_{mid}(z'_1 + DIST) - y'_1 PPD}{(y'_2 - y'_1)PPD - y_{mid}(z'_2 - z'_1)}$$

This enables us to calculate ϕ, and hence $(\hat{x}, \hat{y}, \hat{z})$, which in turn is used to find whether the subsegment of Γ_2 is visible or not.

In the program that follows each line is compared with every facet; at the time before comparing the Ith line with the Jth facet, we assume that NRL visible line segments have been discovered. The μ values for the end points of the Kth visible segment are stored at RM(1, K) and RM(2, K). Initially NRL = 1 and RM(1, 1) = 0 and RM(2, 1) = 1, that is, the complete line is assumed to be visible. Whenever a new hidden segment is discovered, specified by μ_{min} and μ_{max} (RMIN and RMAX), the values in the RM array and NRL are adjusted accordingly.

When all the facets have been compared with the Ith line, we are left with NRL segments that are drawn on the screen. If at any time NRL becomes zero, then the Ith line is completely hidden, and no more comparisons are needed. The programs allow space for a maximum of 50 such subsegments.

```
      SUBROUTINE HIDDEN
C HIDDEN LINE ALGORITHM TO TAKE THE 2-D PERSPECTIVE PICTURE OF 3-D
C SPACE AND CUT THE LINE SEGMENTS IN THE PICTURE INTO VISIBLE AND
C INVISIBLE PARTS, AND THEN DRAW THE VISIBLE PARTS.
      COMMON/VERTS/NOV,X(300),Y(300),Z(300),XP(300),YP(300)
      COMMON/LINES/NOL,LINV(2,400)
      COMMON/FACETS/NOF,INDEXF(200),LINF(6,200)
      COMMON DIST,PPD
      DIMENSION RM(2,50)
      F(XX,YY)=SIGN(1.0,(YY-Y1)*XD-(XX-X1)*YD)
      G(XX,YY)=SIGN(1.0,(YY-Y1)*YD+(XX-X1)*XD)
      H(XX,YY)=SIGN(1.0,(YY-Y2)*YD+(XX-X2)*XD)
C LOOK AT EACH LINE.
      DO 20 I=1,NOL
      L1=LINV(1,I)
      L2=LINV(2,I)
      NRL=1
      RM(1,1)=0.0
      RM(2,1)=1.0
      X1=XP(L1)
      Y1=YP(L1)
      Y2=YP(L2)
      X2=XP(L2)
C (X1,Y1) AND (X2,Y2) ARE THE ENDS OF THE LINE IN 2-D(SCREEN) SPACE.
      XD=X2-X1
      YD=Y2-Y1
C COMPARE I'TH LINE WITH J'TH FACET.
      DO 18 J=1,NOF
      IN=INDEXF(J)
      DO 1 K=1,IN
C IF I'TH LINE LIES IN J'TH FACET THEN EXIT FACET LOOP.
      IF(LINF(K,J).EQ.I) GO TO 18
    1 CONTINUE
C CHECK POSSIBILITY A).
      NN=LINF(1,J)
      IV1=LINV(1,NN)
      FVAL=F(XP(IV1),YP(IV1))
      IF(ABS(FVAL).LT.0.000001) GO TO 3
      DO 2 K=2,IN
      NN=LINF(K,J)
      IV2=LINV(1,NN)
      IF(ABS(FVAL-F(XP(IV2),YP(IV2))).GT.0.000001) GO TO 3
      IV2=LINV(2,NN)
      IF(ABS(FVAL-F(XP(IV2),YP(IV2))).GT.0.000001) GO TO 3
    2 CONTINUE
      GO TO 18
C CHECK POSSIBILITY B).
    3 GVAL=G(X2,Y2)
      IF(ABS(GVAL).LT.0.000001) GO TO 5
      DO 4 K=1,IN
      NN=LINF(K,J)
      IV2=LINV(1,NN)
      IF(ABS(GVAL-G(XP(IV2),YP(IV2))).LT.1.1) GO TO 5
      IV2=LINV(2,NN)
      IF(ABS(GVAL-G(XP(IV2),YP(IV2))).LT.1.1) GO TO 5
    4 CONTINUE
      GO TO 18
C CHECK POSSIBILITY C).
    5 HVAL=H(X1,Y1)
      IF(ABS(HVAL).LT.0.000001) GO TO 7
      DO 6 K=1,IN
      NN=LINF(K,J)
      IV2=LINV(1,NN)
      IF(ABS(HVAL-H(XP(IV2),YP(IV2))).LT.1.1) GO TO 7
      IV2=LINV(2,NN)
      IF(ABS(HVAL-H(XP(IV2),YP(IV2))).LT.1.1) GO TO 7
    6 CONTINUE
      GO TO 18
```

```
C THE NEXT LOOP FINDS THE TWO POINTS OF INTERSECTION OF PROJECTED
C LINE WITH PROJECTED FACET. THESE POINTS ARE SPECIFIED BY MU
C VALUES RMIN AND RMAX.
    7 RMAX=0.0
      RMIN=1.0
      DO 10 K=1,IN
      NN=LINF(K,J)
      IV1=LINV(1,NN)
      IV2=LINV(2,NN)
      XE=XP(IV1)-XP(IV2)
      YE=YP(IV1)-YP(IV2)
      XF=XP(IV1)-X1
      YF=YP(IV1)-Y1
      DISK=XD*YE-XE*YD
      IF(ABS(DISK).GT.0.000001) GO TO 9
C IF THE LINE OVERLAPS A LINE ON THE FACET, THEN LEAVE FACET LOOP.
C ANY OTHER FACET EDGE PARALLEL TO THE LINE, CANNOT CUT THE LINE.
      IF(ABS(XD).GT.0.000001) GO TO 8
      IF(ABS(XF).LT.0.000001) GO TO 18
      GO TO 10
    8 XSI=XF/XD
      IF(ABS(YF-XSI*YD).LT.0.000001) GO TO 18
      GO TO 10
    9 XSI=(XD*YF-YD*XF)/DISK
      IF(XSI.LT.-0.000001) GO TO 10
C IF LINE MISSES FACET THEN EXIT FACET LOOP.
      IF(XSI.GT.1.000001) GO TO 10
      RMU=(YE*XF-XE*YF)/DISK
      IF(RMAX.LT.RMU) RMAX=RMU
      IF(RMIN.GT.RMU) RMIN=RMU
   10 CONTINUE
      IF(RMIN.GT.1.0) GO TO 18
      IF(RMAX.LT.0.0) GO TO 18
      RMAX=AMIN1(1.0,RMAX)
      RMIN=AMAX1(0.0,RMIN)
      IF(RMAX-RMIN.LT.0.000001) GO TO 18
C FIND XMID AND YMID.
      RMID=(RMAX+RMIN)*0.5
      RXX=1.0-RMID
      XMID=RXX*X1+RMID*X2
      YMID=RXX*Y1+RMID*Y2
C FIND XHAT,YHAT AND ZHAT FROM THE VALUE OF PHI.
      DENOM=PPD*(X(L2)-X(L1))-XMID*(Z(L2)-Z(L1))
      IF(ABS(DENOM).LT.0.000001) GO TO 11
      PHI=(XMID*(Z(L1)+DIST)-PPD*X(L1))/DENOM
      GO TO 12
   11 DENOM=PPD*(Y(L2)-Y(L1))-YMID*(Z(L2)-Z(L1))
      PHI=(YMID*(Z(L1)+DIST)-PPD*Y(L1))/DENOM
   12 ZHAT=(1.0-PHI)*Z(L1)+PHI*Z(L2)
      DDD=(ZHAT+DIST)/PPD
      XHAT=XMID*DDD
      YHAT=YMID*DDD
C CALCULATE COEFFICIENTS OF THE PLANE    A.X+B.Y+C.Z=D .
      I1=LINF(1,J)
      I2=LINF(2,J)
      IV1=LINV(1,I1)
      IV2=LINV(2,I1)
      IV3=LINV(1,I2)
      IF(IV1.EQ.IV3.OR.IV2.EQ.IV3) IV3=LINV(2,I2)
      DX1=X(IV1)-X(IV2)
      DY1=Y(IV1)-Y(IV2)
      DZ1=Z(IV1)-Z(IV2)
      DZ3=Z(IV3)-Z(IV2)
      DY3=Y(IV3)-Y(IV2)
      DX3=X(IV3)-X(IV2)
      A=DY1*DZ3-DY3*DZ1
      B=DZ1*DX3-DZ3*DX1
      C=DX1*DY3-DX3*DY1
```

```
      D=A*X(IV1)+B*Y(IV1)+C*Z(IV1)
      F1=A*XHAT+B*YHAT+C*ZHAT-D
      F2=-DIST*C-D
      IF(ABS(F1).LT.0.000001) GO TO 18
      IF(ABS(SIGN(1.0,F1)-SIGN(1.0,F2)).LT.1.000001) GO TO 18
      MORERL=NRL
C PART OF THE LINE IS HIDDEN SO ALTER THE ARRAY RL.
      DO 16 K=1,NRL
      R1=RM(1,K)
      R2=RM(2,K)
      IF(R1.GT.RMAX.OR.R2.LT.RMIN) GO TO 16
      IF(R1.GE.RMIN.AND.R2.LE.RMAX) GO TO 15
      IF(R1.LT.RMIN.AND.R2.GT.RMAX) GO TO 13
      IF(R1.LT.RMIN) GO TO 14
      RM(1,K)=RMAX
      GO TO 16
   13 MORERL=MORERL+1
      RM(1,MORERL)=RMAX
      RM(2,MORERL)=R2
   14 RM(2,K)=RMIN
      GO TO 16
   15 RM(1,K)=-1.0
   16 CONTINUE
      NRL=0
C TIDY UP THE ARRAY RL AFTER IT HAS BEEN ALTERED.
      DO 17 K=1,MORERL
      IF(RM(1,K).LT.-0.000001) GO TO 17
      NRL=NRL+1
      RM(1,NRL)=RM(1,K)
      RM(2,NRL)=RM(2,K)
   17 CONTINUE
      IF(NRL.EQ.0) GO TO 20
   18 CONTINUE
C DRAW VISIBLE PARTS OF THE I'TH LINE (IF ANY).
      DO 19 J=1,NRL
      R1=RM(1,J)
      R2=1.0-R1
      XP1=X1*R2+X2*R1
      YP1=Y1*R2+Y2*R1
      R1=RM(2,J)
      R2=1.0-R1
      XP2=X1*R2+X2*R1
      YP2=Y1*R2+Y2*R1
      IF(ABS(XP1-XP2).LT.0.000001.AND.ABS(YP1-YP2).LT.0.000001) GO TO 19
      CALL PLOT(XP1,YP1,3)
      CALL PLOT(XP2,YP2,2)
   19 CONTINUE
   20 CONTINUE
      RETURN
      END
```

Program 8.5

| 1 INCH |

Figure 8.2

Example 8.2

Draw figure 8.2, an example of an interpenetrant cubic crystal.

The program to draw this figure uses programs 8.2 and 8.5, together with the following SETUP routine

```
      SUBROUTINE SETUP
C SUBROUTINE TO SETUP AN INTERPENETRANT CUBIC CRYSTAL. DATA IS READ
C FROM THE DATA FILE TAPE2 - VERTEX ENTRIES WITH INDICES 15 TO 20 ARE
C THREE TIMES TOO BIG. IT IS EASIER TO DIVIDE BY 3 IN THE PROGRAM
C THAN TO INTRODUCE SUFFICIENT ACCURACY IN THE DATA.
      COMMON/VERTS/NOV,X(300),Y(300),Z(300),XP(300),YP(300)
      COMMON/LINES/NOL,LINV(2,400)
      COMMON/FACETS/NOF,INDEXF(200),LINF(6,200)
      COMMON DIST,PPD
      READ(2,1) NOV
    1 FORMAT(I2)
      READ(2,*) ((X(I),Y(I),Z(I)),I=1,NOV)
      DO 2 KK=15,20
      X(KK)=X(KK)/3.0
      Y(KK)=Y(KK)/3.0
      Z(KK)=Z(KK)/3.0
    2 CONTINUE
      READ(2,1) NOL
      READ(2,*) ((LINV(1,I),LINV(2,I)),I=1,NOL)
      READ(2,1) NOF
      READ(2,*) ((LINF(J,I),J=1,3),I=1,NOF)
      DO 3 I=1,NOF
      INDEXF(I)=3
    3 CONTINUE
      RETURN
      END
```

Program 8.6

which reads data from an input file on the data channel TAPE2. Study these values!

```
20  VERTICES
  1.0     1.0     1.0    -1.0     1.0     1.0
 -1.0    -1.0     1.0     1.0    -1.0     1.0
 -1.0    -1.0    -1.0     1.0    -1.0    -1.0
  1.0     1.0    -1.0    -1.0     1.0    -1.0
 -1.0     0.0     1.0     0.0    -1.0     1.0
  1.0    -1.0     0.0     1.0     0.0    -1.0
  0.0     1.0    -1.0    -1.0     1.0     0.0
  5.0    -1.0    -1.0    -1.0     5.0    -1.0
 -1.0    -1.0     5.0    -5.0     1.0     1.0
  1.0    -5.0     1.0     1.0     1.0    -5.0
54  LINES
  1   2,   4   1,   1   7,   3   5,   8   5,   5   6,   2   9,   9   3,   3  10,  10   4
  4  11,  11   6,   6  12,  12   7,   7  13,  13   8,   8  14,  14   2,   9  10,  10  11
 11  12,  12  13,  13  14,  14   9,   1   9,   1  10,   1  11,   1  12,   1  13,   1  14
  5   9,   5  10,   5  11,   5  12,   5  13,   5  14,  15   1,  15  11,  15  12,  16   1
 16  13,  16  14,  17   1,  17   9,  17  10,  18   5,  18  14,  18   9,  19   5,  19  10
 19  11,  20   5,  20  12,  20  13
36  FACETS
  2  11  27,  13  21  12,   3  14  28,   3  15  29,  17  23  16,   1  18  30
  1   7  25,   9  19   8,   2  10  26,   5  17  36,   7  24  18,   4   8  31
  4   9  32,  11  20  10,   6  12  33,   6  13  34,  15  22  14,   5  16  35
 37  27  38,  38  21  39,  39  28  37,  40  29  41,  41  23  42,  42  30  40
 43  25  44,  44  19  45,  45  26  43,  46  36  47,  47  24  48,  48  31  46
 49  32  50,  50  20  51,  51  33  49,  52  34  53,  53  22  54,  54  35  52
```

Program 8.7

Exercise 8.3
Produce a general orthographic Hidden Line Algorithm.

Exercise 8.4
Draw a diagram similar to figure 8.3, the SETUP space being two cubes
($\pm 1, \pm 1, \pm 1$) and ($\frac{1}{2}, \frac{1}{2}, 2$) + ($\pm 1, \pm 1, \pm 1$). This was viewed from (5, 10, −15) with
PPD = 33.

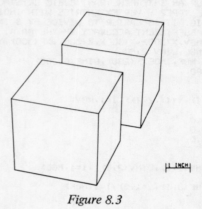

|⊢ INCH⊣|

Figure 8.3

Exercise 8.5
Produce a general stereoscopic Hidden Line Algorithm.

9 Setup Techniques

Thus far we have concentrated on well-defined and simple individual objects in three-dimensional space, so as not to confuse the descriptions of transformations between SETUP, ACTUAL and OBSERVER triads, of orthographic, perspective and stereoscopic projections, and of the Hidden Line Algorithms. The scope for these kind of figures is rather limited, and therefore far more complicated constructions must be considered.

To do this, we totally reorganise the ideas introduced in the earlier chapters. The OBSERVE routine stays in its original form, but now it is the first routine called, and as usual it returns the ACTUAL—OBSERVER matrix Q. Since we are dealing with possibly a large number of objects, each will be given its own unique SETUP—ACTUAL matrix P and, rather than clutter the program with a number of ACTUAL subroutines, we will not explicitly create them.

The SETUP routine will have Q as an input parameter, and it will initially set the values of NOV, NOL and NOF to zero. Then follow a number of sections, one for each object to be defined. Each section will be in two parts. The first is a series of statements that are equivalent to the ACTUAL subroutine, producing a SETUP—ACTUAL matrix P. The second part creates the SETUP—OBSERVER matrix $R = Q \times P$, and inputs it into a subroutine, together with any other relevant information. The routine, which is called a 'building brick', produces the SETUP information on the object (vertex, line and facet data), and then transforms the vertex data using the matrix R so that the object is 'moved' to its required position in OBSERVER space (that is, relative to the OBSERVER triad of axes). These values are added to the COMMON stores /VERTS/, /LINES/ and /FACETS/, the transformed vertices are added to the X, Y and Z arrays, the lines to the LINV array, and the facets to the INDEXF and LINF arrays. The NOV, NOL and NOF values are incremented accordingly; also the perspective projections of the vertices are stored in the XP and YP arrays.

The information on the individual objects is created using methods we have already seen: reading information from data files, DATA statements and by direct calculation. The 'building-brick' method is illustrated by a 'brick' subroutine RECT, which forms a rectangular block of dimension 2A × 2B × 2C screen inches, placed in OBSERVER space by the matrix R.

```
      SUBROUTINE RECT(R,A,B,C)
C ROUTINE TO SETUP A RECTANGULAR BLOCK 2A X 2B X 2C IN OBSERVER SPACE.
C SETUP TO OBSERVER MATRIX IS R.
      COMMON/VERTS/NOV,X(300),Y(300),Z(300),XP(300),YP(300)
      COMMON/LINES/NOL,LINV(2,400)
      COMMON/FACETS/NOF,INDEXF(200),LINF(6,200)
      COMMON DIST,PPD
      DIMENSION XX(8),YY(8),ZZ(8),LV(2,12),LF(4,6),R(4,4)
C XX,YY,ZZ,LV,LF HOLD SETUP INFORMATION FOR A SIMPLE CUBE.
C THIS WILL BE EXTENDED TO DRAW A GENERAL RECTANGULAR BLOCK.
      DATA XX/1.0,1.0,1.0,1.0,-1.0,-1.0,-1.0,-1.0/
      DATA YY/1.0,-1.0,1.0,-1.0,1.0,-1.0,1.0,-1.0/
      DATA ZZ/1.0,1.0,-1.0,-1.0,1.0,1.0,-1.0,-1.0/
      DATA LV/1,2,2,4,4,3,3,1,5,6,6,8,8,7,7,5,1,5,2,6,4,8,3,7/
      DATA LF/1,2,3,4,5,6,7,8,1,10,5,9,2,11,6,10,3,12,7,11,4,9,8,12/
C ADD VERTICES IN OBSERVER SPACE AND PROJECTIONS TO /VERTS/ LIST.
      DO 1 I=1,8
      INOV=I+NOV
      X(INOV)=A*R(1,1)*XX(I)+B*R(1,2)*YY(I)+C*R(1,3)*ZZ(I)+R(1,4)
      Y(INOV)=A*R(2,1)*XX(I)+B*R(2,2)*YY(I)+C*R(2,3)*ZZ(I)+R(2,4)
      Z(INOV)=A*R(3,1)*XX(I)+B*R(3,2)*YY(I)+C*R(3,3)*ZZ(I)+R(3,4)
      DD=PPD/(Z(INOV)+DIST)
      XP(INOV)=X(INOV)*DD
      YP(INOV)=Y(INOV)*DD
    1 CONTINUE
C ADD LINES TO /LINES/ LIST.
      DO 2 I=1,12
      INOL=I+NOL
      LINV(1,INOL)=LV(1,I)+NOV
      LINV(2,INOL)=LV(2,I)+NOV
    2 CONTINUE
C ADD TO /FACETS/ LIST.
      DO 4 I=1,6
      INOF=I+NOF
      INDEXF(INOF)=4
      DO 3 J=1,4
      LINF(J,INOF)=LF(J,I)+NOL
    3 CONTINUE
    4 CONTINUE
C INCREASE THE VERTEX, LINE AND FACET COUNT.
      NOV=NOV+8
      NOL=NOL+12
      NOF=NOF+6
      RETURN
      END
```

Program 9.1

Exercise 9.1

Produce a 'brick' routine PYRMID, which forms a pyramid with a rectangular base 2A × 2C and height B in SETUP space and places it in OBSERVER space using a matrix *R*.

Example 9.1

Draw figure 9.1, a hidden line picture of two pyramids placed on a rectangular block, viewed from (15, 20, 25) with PPD = 33.

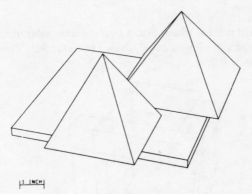

|1 INCH|

Figure 9.1

The routines RECT and PYRMID are called from the SETUP routine (program 9.3), which in turn is called from the Main Program 9.2 to draw the figure.

```
      COMMON DIST,PPD
      DIMENSION Q(4,4)
C CALCULATE THE OBSERVATION MATRIX Q
      CALL OBSERVE(Q)
      WRITE(6,1)
    1 FORMAT(* TYPE IN DISTANCE OF EYE FROM PERSPECTIVE PLANE*)
      READ(5,*) PPD
      CALL START(2)
      CALL PLOT(9.5,7.375,-3)
      CALL SETUP(Q)
      CALL HIDDEN
```

Program 9.2

```
      SUBROUTINE SETUP(Q)
C ROUTINE TO SETUP TWO PYRAMIDS ON A THIN RECTANGULAR 'TABLETOP'.
      DIMENSION P(4,4),Q(4,4),R(4,4)
      COMMON/VERTS/NOV,X(300),Y(300),Z(300),XP(300),YP(300)
      COMMON/LINES/NOL,LINV(2,400)
      COMMON/FACETS/NOF,INDEXF(200),LINF(6,200)
      NOL=0
      NOV=0
      NOF=0
C PLACE THE TABLETOP - P IS THE IDENTITY MATRIX, THUS R=Q.
      CALL RECT(Q,4.0,0.2,4.0)
C PLACE THE FIRST PYRAMID.
      CALL TRAN(2.0,-0.2,-2.0,P)
      CALL MULT(Q,P,R)
      CALL PYRMID(R,2.5,4.0,2.5)
C PLACE SECOND PYRAMID.
      CALL TRAN(-3.0,-0.2,0.0,P)
      CALL MULT(Q,P,R)
      CALL PYRMID(R,2.0,4.0,2.0)
      RETURN
      END
```

Program 9.3

Sometimes the 'bricks' are not placed in arbitrary positions and orientations in space; they may be closely interrelated — as in the next example.

Example 9.2

Produce the SETUP routine which places twelve rectangular blocks and eight cubes in the form of a 'hollowed cube', shown in figure 9.2. Viewpoint is (10, 20, 30) and PPD = 25

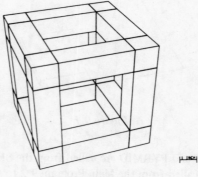

Figure 9.2

We use the RECT routine of program 9.1 as follows.

```
      SUBROUTINE SETUP(Q)
C SETUP A HOLLOWED CUBE. Q IS THE ACTUAL TO OBSERVER MATRIX.
C EACH PIECE OF THE FIGURE HAS ITS OWN SETUP TO ACTUAL MATRIX P,
C WHICH IS GENERATED IN THIS ROUTINE - NOT IN INDIVIDUAL ACTUAL
C ROUTINES. THE SETUP TO OBSERVER MATRIX R IS CALCULATED FOR EACH
C PIECE OF THE FINAL FIGURE.
      DIMENSION P(4,4),Q(4,4),R(4,4),XX(8),YY(8),ZZ(8)
      COMMON/VERTS/NOV,X(300),Y(300),Z(300),XP(300),YP(300)
      COMMON/LINES/NOL,LINV(2,400)
      COMMON/FACETS/NOF,INDEXF(200),LINF(6,200)
C XX,YY,ZZ HOLD INFORMATION TO BE USED IN PLACING THE 20 BLOCKS.
      DATA XX/1.0,1.0,1.0,1.0,-1.0,-1.0,-1.0,-1.0/
      DATA YY/1.0,1.0,-1.0,-1.0,1.0,1.0,-1.0,-1.0/
      DATA ZZ/1.0,-1.0,1.0,-1.0,1.0,-1.0,1.0,-1.0/
      NOL=0
      NOV=0
      NOF=0
C SETUP 12 RECTANGULAR BLOCKS WHICH JOIN THE CORNER CUBES.
      DO 1 I=1,4
      CALL TRAN(0.0,4.0*YY(I),4.0*ZZ(I),P)
      CALL MULT(Q,P,R)
      CALL RECT(R,3.0,1.0,1.0)
      CALL TRAN(4.0*ZZ(I),0.0,4.0*YY(I),P)
      CALL MULT(Q,P,R)
      CALL RECT(R,1.0,3.0,1.0)
      CALL TRAN(4.0*YY(I),4.0*ZZ(I),0.0,P)
      CALL MULT(Q,P,R)
      CALL RECT(R,1.0,1.0,3.0)
    1 CONTINUE
C SETUP THE 8 CORNER CUBES.
      DO 2 I=1,8
      CALL TRAN(4.0*XX(I),4.0*YY(I),4.0*ZZ(I),P)
      CALL MULT(Q,P,R)
      CALL RECT(R,1.0,1.0,1.0)
    2 CONTINUE
      RETURN
      END
```

Program 9.4

Note how a DATA statement is used to introduce information that can be used to calculate the positions of the various 'bricks'. The figure is drawn by using program 9.2 to call the SETUP routine of program 9.4.

Exercise 9.2
Some of the vertices, lines and facets created in the last SETUP routine are duplicated. If a facet is common to two separate 'bricks', then the vertices and lines on the facet, as well as the facet itself (which is necessarily hidden), will each be specified by two different indices. Write a general-purpose CLEANUP routine that will delete all redundant information from the COMMON stores /VERTS/, /LINES/ and /FACETS/. *Note* The doubly indicated lines will be drawn twice; this is why some lines in figure 9.2 appear darker than the rest.

THE USE OF 'BRICKS' TO BUILD 'HOUSING ESTATES'

One of the most important uses of computer graphics is in architectural design and planning. There are a number of sophisticated (and expensive!) computer packages commercially available that deal with these problems. However, the ideas behind these computer libraries are basically those given in this book. Naturally there is a great deal of specialisation and complexity in the SETUP of objects, but they nevertheless reduce to the simple ideas we are discussing.

Example 9.3
Use these techniques to create an outline of an idealised and simplified house, and then produce a hidden line perspective picture of an estate of houses similar to the four in figure 9.3.

```
      SUBROUTINE SETUP(Q)
C ROUTINE TO SET UP A SIMPLE HOUSING ESTATE OF 4 HOUSES.
      DIMENSION P(4,4),Q(4,4),R(4,4),S(4,4)
      COMMON/VERTS/NOV,X(300),Y(300),Z(300),XP(300),YP(300)
      COMMON/LINES/NOL,LINV(2,400)
      COMMON/FACETS/NOF,INDEXF(200),LINF(6,200)
      NOL=0
      NOV=0
      NOF=0
      CALL TRAN(0.0,0.0,12.0,P)
      CALL MULT(Q,P,R)
      CALL HOUSE(R)
      PI=3.1415926535
      PI2=PI*0.5
      CALL ROT(2,-PI2,R)
      CALL TRAN(12.0,0.0,0.0,S)
      CALL MULT(S,R,P)
      CALL MULT(Q,P,R)
      CALL HOUSE(R)
      CALL ROT(2,PI,R)
      CALL TRAN(0.0,0.0,-12.0,S)
      CALL MULT(S,R,P)
      CALL MULT(Q,P,R)
      CALL HOUSE(R)
      CALL ROT(2,PI2,R)
      CALL TRAN(-12.0,0.0,0.0,S)
      CALL MULT(S,R,P)
      CALL MULT(Q,P,R)
      CALL HOUSE(R)
      RETURN
      END                        Program 9.5
```

```
      SUBROUTINE HOUSE (R)
C ROUTINE TO SETUP AN IDEALISED HOUSE AND POSITION IT IN OBSERVER
C SPACE USING MATRIX R.
      COMMON/VERTS/NOV,X(300),Y(300),Z(300),XP(300),YP(300)
      COMMON/LINES/NOL,LINV(2,400)
      COMMON/FACETS/NOF,INDEXF(200),LINF(6,200)
      COMMON DIST,PPD
      DIMENSION IX(59),IY(59),IZ(59),LV(2,62),LF(5,6),R(4,4)
      DATA IX/6,-6,-6,6,6,-6,-6,6,-6,6,4,1,1,4,-4,-1,-1,-4,4,1,1,4,
     +      0,0,-5,-5,-6,-6,-6,-6,-6,-5,-2,-2,-5,5,2,2,5,-5,-2,-2,-5,
     +      5,2,2,5,1,1,0,-1,-1,6,6,6,6,6,6,6/
      DATA IY/0,0,0,0,8,8,8,8,11,11,7,7,5,5,7,7,5,5,3,3,1,1,0,3,3,0,
     +      7,7,5,5,7,7,5,5,7,7,5,5,3,3,1,1,3,3,1,1,0,3,4,3,0,7,7,
     +      5,5,0,3,3,0/
      DATA IZ/4,4,-4,-4,4,4,-4,-4,0,0,4,4,4,4,4,4,4,4,4,4,4,4,4,4,4,4,
     +      -3,-1,-1,-3,-4,-4,-4,-4,-4,-4,-4,-4,-4,-4,-4,-4,-4,-4,-4,
     +      -4,-4,-4,-4,-4,-4,3,1,1,3,1,1,3,3/
      DATA LV/1,2,2,3,3,4,4,1,5,6,6,9,9,7,7,8,8,10,10,5,1,5,2,6,3,7,
     +      4,8,9,10,11,12,12,13,13,14,14,11,15,16,16,17,17,18,18,
     +      15,19,20,20,21,21,22,22,19,23,24,24,25,25,26,26,23,27,
     +      28,28,29,29,30,30,27,31,32,32,33,33,34,34,31,35,36,36,
     +      37,37,38,38,35,39,40,40,41,41,42,42,39,43,44,44,45,45,
     +      46,46,43,47,48,48,49,49,50,50,51,52,53,53,54,54,55,55,
     +      52,56,57,57,58,58,59/
      DATA LF/1,12,5,11,0,2,13,7,6,12,3,14,8,13,0,4,11,10,9,14,
     +      8,9,15,7,0,5,6,15,10,0/
      DO 1 I=1,59
      INOV=I+NOV
      X(INOV)=R(1,1)*IX(I)+R(1,2)*IY(I)+R(1,3)*IZ(I)+R(1,4)
      Y(INOV)=R(2,1)*IX(I)+R(2,2)*IY(I)+R(2,3)*IZ(I)+R(2,4)
      Z(INOV)=R(3,1)*IX(I)+R(3,2)*IY(I)+R(3,3)*IZ(I)+R(3,4)
      DD=PPD/(DIST+Z(INOV))
      XP(INOV)=X(INOV)*DD
      YP(INOV)=Y(INOV)*DD
    1 CONTINUE
      DO 2 I=1,62
      INOL=I+NOL
      LINV(1,INOL)=LV(1,I)+NOV
      LINV(2,INOL)=LV(2,I)+NOV
    2 CONTINUE
      DO 4 I=1,6
      INOF=I+NOF
      INDEXF(INOF)=4
      DO 3 J=1,5
      LINF(J,INOF)=LF(J,I)+NOL
    3 CONTINUE
    4 CONTINUE
      INDEXF(NOF+2)=5
      INDEXF(NOF+4)=5
      NOV=NOV+59
      NOL=NOL+62
      NOF=NOF+6
      RETURN
      END
```

Program 9.6

Program 9.2 may be used to call the SETUP routine, program 9.5, which in turn uses the 'brick' subroutine, program 9.6. As usual, the OBSERVE routine sets the matrix Q from the ACTUAL coordinates of the observation point (EX, EY, EZ). Note that some of the lines are not edges of a facet; they simply lie on the surface of a facet, for example, the outlines of the windows and doors.

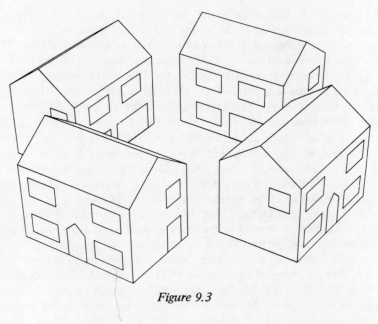

Figure 9.3

Exercise 9.3
Study the way that the coordinates of the vertices, lines and facets of figure 9.3
are generated. Add extra information: put on chimney stacks, curtains in the
windows, etc.

Exercise 9.4
Draw an industrial estate — warehouses, office blocks, etc. Introduce a paved
ground level by adding a flat rectangular grid on which the buildings will stand.

We now introduce a special form of 'brick', a 'body of rotation'. We consider
two types: skeleton bodies and solid bodies.

SKELETON BODIES OF ROTATION

The Hidden Line Algorithms are not used in this type of body, instead we
concentrate on 'wire skeletons'.

The method requires a sequence of NLVERT lines (called the first vertical
sequence) in the $z = 0$ plane of SETUP space, that is, relative to the SETUP axes.
These lines are defined by the NLVERT + 1 (= NOPTS) vertices
$\{$(XLIN(I), YLIN(I), 0) | I = 1, . . . , NOPTS and XLIN(I) $\geqslant$ 0 for all I$\}$. These
are the end points of the lines taken in order, that is, the Ith line joins
(XLIN(I), YLIN(I), 0) to (XLIN(I + 1), YLIN(I + 1), 0). We think of the planes

parallel to the $y = 0$ plane as horizontal, and all lines perpendicular to the horizontal are called vertical — whence the first vertical sequence.

This first vertical sequence is rotated about the y-axis by an angle 2π/NHORIZ radians. Repeating the rotation NHORIZ times produces a set of NHORIZ vertical sequences surrounding the vertical axis. Thus the Ith defining point on the first vertical sequence, (XLIN(I), YLIN(I), 0), is rotated into NHORIZ points on the horizontal plane y = YLIN(I) (we call this the Ith level), $\{$(XLIN(I) cos θ, YLIN(I), XLIN(I) sin θ) $| \; \theta = 2\pi(J - 1)$/NHORIZ; J = 1, . . . , NHORIZ$\}$. These are joined in order to form a regular polygon with NHORIZ sides on this Ith horizontal level. We thus have NOPTS horizontal sequences; however, if XLIN(I) = 0 for any value of I, then the regular polygon degenerates to the point where the y-axis cuts the Ith level. The complete set of vertical and horizontal lines formed in this way produces the surface of a skeleton body.

Since we are not considering hidden lines there is no need to store facet information; in fact, if we only wish to draw a single figure there is no need to store all the lines and vertices! This is the simple case we describe.

We produce consecutive vertical sequences; each point on a sequence, (XA, YA, ZA) say, is transformed by the SETUP—OBSERVER matrix R to the point (XB, YB, ZB) in OBSERVER space, which in turn is perspectively projected into a point on the screen. At any one time, two consecutive vertical sequences are transformed in this way to produce the (XPRES, YPRES) and (XNEXT, YNEXT) arrays. The vertical lines of the XPRES, YPRES sequence are drawn together with the horizontal lines between the two sequences, provided the line does not degenerate to a point on the vertical axis of SETUP space. Thus, the complete skeleton body can be drawn inside the subroutine ROTBOD (program 9.7) and *not* in the Main Program or in a HIDDEN routine as in previous programs.

```
      SUBROUTINE ROTBOD(NOPTS,NHORIZ,R,XLIN,YLIN)
C ROUTINE TO DRAW SKELETON BODY OF ROTATION.
C R IS THE SETUP TO OBSERVER MATRIX.
      DIMENSION R(4,4),XLIN(100),YLIN(100)
      DIMENSION XNEXT(100),YNEXT(100),XPRES(100),YPRES(100)
      COMMON DIST,PPD
      THDIF=6.283185307/FLOAT(NHORIZ)
      THETA=0.0
C SETUP FIRST VERTICAL SEQUENCE OF VERTICES.
      DO 1 I=1,NOPTS
      XB=R(1,1)*XLIN(I)+R(1,2)*YLIN(I)+R(1,4)
      YB=R(2,1)*XLIN(I)+R(2,2)*YLIN(I)+R(2,4)
      ZB=R(3,1)*XLIN(I)+R(3,2)*YLIN(I)+R(3,4)+DIST
      XPRES(I)=XB*PPD/ZB
      YPRES(I)=YB*PPD/ZB
    1 CONTINUE
C PASS THROUGH ALL VERTICAL SEQUENCES.
      DO 5 J=1,NHORIZ
C DRAW PRESENT VERTICAL SEQUENCE.
      CALL PLOT(XPRES(1),YPRES(1),3)
      DO 2 I=2,NOPTS
      CALL PLOT(XPRES(I),YPRES(I),2)
    2 CONTINUE
      THETA=THETA+THDIF
      CT=COS(THETA)
      ST=SIN(THETA)
```

```
C CALCULATE NEXT VERTICAL SEQUENCE OF VERTICES.
      DO 4 I=1,NOPTS
      XA=XLIN(I)*CT
      YA=YLIN(I)
      ZA=XLIN(I)*ST
      XB=R(1,1)*XA+R(1,2)*YA+R(1,3)*ZA+R(1,4)
      YB=R(2,1)*XA+R(2,2)*YA+R(2,3)*ZA+R(2,4)
      ZB=R(3,1)*XA+R(3,2)*YA+R(3,3)*ZA+R(3,4)+DIST
      XNEXT(I)=XB*PPD/ZB
      YNEXT(I)=YB*PPD/ZB
C PLOT HORIZONTAL LINES BETWEEN PRESENT AND NEXT SEQUENCES.
      IF(ABS(XLIN(I)).LT.0.000001) GO TO 3
      CALL PLOT(XPRES(I),YPRES(I),3)
      CALL PLOT(XNEXT(I),YNEXT(I),2)
C RESET PRESENT SEQUENCE TO NEXT SEQUENCE.
    3 XPRES(I)=XNEXT(I)
      YPRES(I)=YNEXT(I)
    4 CONTINUE
    5 CONTINUE
      RETURN
      END
```

Program 9.7

Example 9.4

Draw the skeleton spheroid shown in figure 9.4. The observation point is
(15, 20, 25) and PPD = 33; the radius of the spheroid is 4 screen inches.

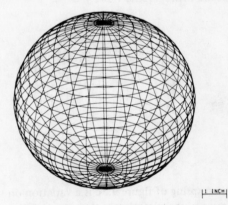

Figure 9.4

In fact the program we give generates a skeleton ellipsoid; the major and
minor axes of the figure, A and B, are read in from the keyboard. A SETUP
routine (program 9.8) generates a semi-ellipse in the XLIN and YLIN arrays,
before calling the ROTBOD routine. Since there is only one figure, and the
COMMON stores /VERTS/, etc., are not required, the NOV, NOL and NOF
values are not initialised. The figure is drawn by a Main Program similar to
program 9.2; however, the call to HIDDEN is deleted.

```
      SUBROUTINE SETUP (Q)
C ROUTINE TO SETUP FIRST VERTICAL SEQUENCE OF AN ELLIPSOID.
      DIMENSION Q(4,4),XLIN(100),YLIN(100)
      WRITE(6,1)
    1 FORMAT(* TYPE IN NO. OF LINES IN VERTICAL AND HORIZONTAL SEQUENCES
     +*)
      READ(5,*) NLVERT,NHORIZ
      NOPTS=NLVERT+1
      PI=3.1415926535
      PH=-PI*0.5
      PHDIF=PI/FLOAT(NLVERT)
      WRITE(6,2)
    2 FORMAT(* TYPE MAJOR AND MINOR AXES *)
      READ(5,*) A,B
C CREATE FIRST VERTICAL SEQUENCE.
      DO 3 I=1,NOPTS
      XLIN(I)=A*COS(PH)
      YLIN(I)=B*SIN(PH)
      PH=PH+PHDIF
    3 CONTINUE
C ACTUAL SPACE IS IDENTIFIED WITH SETUP SPACE THEREFORE THE
C SETUP TO ACTUAL MATRIX R IS IDENTICAL TO MATRIX Q.
C DRAW THE SKELETON BODY OF ROTATION IN OBSERVER SPACE.
      CALL ROTBOD(NOPTS,NHORIZ,Q,XLIN,YLIN)
      RETURN
      END
```

Program 9.8

Exercise 9.5
Practise this technique by drawing the washer, cap and spring shown in figure 9.5. (Note that these are orthographic views.)

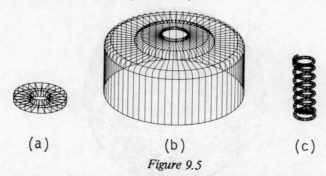

(a)   (b)   (c)

Figure 9.5

Note that the coiled spring of figure 9.5c is a variation on the above technique. The first vertical sequence completes more than one rotation around the vertical axis, and with each small rotation the y-values of the sequence are altered; they do not stay fixed at the YLIN(I) values as they did in the ROTBOD subroutine.

Usually we require that the hidden lines in an object are not seen, and this leads us to the second 'body of rotation' method.

SOLID BODIES OF ROTATION

We proceed in the same way as with the skeleton body, using the same terminology. Now the surface of the body must be stored as facets, and of course lines and vertices, in order to use our Hidden Line Algorithms. We initially rotate the first vertex of the first vertical sequence about the y-axis to produce the lines and vertices on the first horizontal level. If the vertex is on the central axis, then the lines degenerate. We then pass through the horizontal levels, storing the lines (if any) and vertices as they are created, as well as the vertical lines between the present and preceding levels. The facets are calculated as being quadrilateral or triangular areas lying on the surface of the body between the present and preceding levels. They are quadrilateral when the vertices on the two levels are not on the central axis. If the preceding vertices lie on the axis, we get an 'upward' triangular facet; if the present level degenerates, we get a 'downward' triangular facet. This simple approach enables us to define the order of the indices of the vertices in an elementary way, and thence the indices of the lines and facets. The method is given in the listing of the subroutine ROTSOL (program 9.9), which can use either of the HIDDEN routines (programs 8.3 and 8.5) if the final object is convex; program 8.5 must be used with non-convex bodies.

```
      SUBROUTINE ROTSOL (NLVERT,NHORIZ,R,XLIN,YLIN)
C ROUTINE TO SETUP A SOLID BODY OF ROTATION AND PLACE IT IN OBSERVER
C SPACE USING MATRIX R. XLIN, YLIN HOLD THE COORDINATES OF THE FIRST
C VERTICAL SEQUENCE. NLVERT LINES PER VERTICAL SEQUENCE AND NHORIZ
C LINES PER HORIZONTAL SEQUENCE MAKE UP THE SOLID BODY SURFACE.
      COMMON/VERTS/NOV,X(300),Y(300),Z(300),XP(300),YP(300)
      COMMON/LINES/NOL,LINV(2,400)
      COMMON/FACETS/NOF,INDEXF(200),LINF(6,200)
      COMMON DIST,PPD
      DIMENSION R(4,4),XLIN(50),YLIN(50)
C NVBPL = NUMBER OF VERTICES STORED BEFORE THOSE ON PRECEDING LEVEL.
C NLUIPL = NUMBER OF LINES STORED UP TO AND INCLUDING PRECEDING LEVEL.
C LASTV = NUMBER OF VERTICES ON PRECEDING LEVEL.
C NOWV = NUMBER OF VERTICES ON PRESENT LEVEL.
C IF NOWV = 1, THE HORIZONTAL LINES ON PRESENT LEVEL DEGENERATE.
      TDIF=3.1415926535*2.0/FLOAT(NHORIZ)
      NOWV=1
      IF (ABS(XLIN(1)).GT.0.000001) NOWV=NHORIZ
      NVBPL=NOV
      NLUIPL=NOL
      THETA=0.0
C ROTATE AROUND FIRST HORIZONTAL LEVEL.
      DO 1 I=1,NOWV
      XX=XLIN(1)*COS(THETA)
      YY=YLIN(1)
      ZZ=XLIN(1)*SIN(THETA)
      NOV=NOV+1
C SETUP VERTICES ON FIRST LEVEL.
      X(NOV)=XX*R(1,1)+YY*R(1,2)+ZZ*R(1,3)+R(1,4)
      Y(NOV)=XX*R(2,1)+YY*R(2,2)+ZZ*R(2,3)+R(2,4)
      Z(NOV)=XX*R(3,1)+YY*R(3,2)+ZZ*R(3,3)+R(3,4)
      DD=PPD/(DIST+Z(NOV))
      XP(NOV)=X(NOV)*DD
      YP(NOV)=Y(NOV)*DD
      THETA=THETA+TDIF
C SETUP HORIZONTAL LINES ON THIS LEVEL.
      NOL=NOL+1
      LINV(1,NOL)=NVBPL+I
      LINV(2,NOL)=NVBPL+MOD(I,NOWV)+1
    1 CONTINUE
C IF LINES DEGENERATE, DELETE FROM LIST BY RESETING LINE COUNT.
      IF(NOWV.EQ.1) NOL=NOL-1
```

```
C PASS THROUGH HORIZONTAL LEVELS.
      DO 7 I=1,NLVERT
      LASTV=NOWV
      YY=YLIN(I+1)
      XXX=XLIN(I+1)
      NOWV=1
      IF (ABS(XXX .GT.0.000001) NOWV=NHORIZ
      THETA=0.0
C ROTATE AROUND PRESENT HORIZONTAL LEVEL AND SETUP VERTICES.
      DO 2 J=1,NOWV
      XX=XXX*COS(THETA)
      ZZ=XXX*SIN(THETA)
      NOV=NOV+1
      X(NOV)=XX*R(1,1)+YY*R(1,2)+ZZ*R(1,3)+R(1,4)
      Y(NOV)=XX*R(2,1)+YY*R(2,2)+ZZ*R(2,3)+R(2,4)
      Z(NOV)=XX*R(3,1)+YY*R(3,2)+ZZ*R(3,3)+R(3,4)
      DD=PPD/(DIST+Z(NOV))
      XP(NOV)=X(NOV)*DD
      YP(NOV)=Y(NOV)*DD
      THETA=THETA+TDIF
    2 CONTINUE
      DO 3 J=1,NHORIZ
      NOL=NOL+1
C SETUP VERTICAL LINES BETWEEN PRECEDING AND PRESENT LEVELS.
      LINV(1,NOL)=NVBPL+MOD(J-1,LASTV)+1
      LINV(2,NOL)=NVBPL+LASTV+MOD(J-1,NOWV)+1
C SETUP HORIZONTAL LINES ON PRESENT LEVEL.
      LINV(1,NOL+NHORIZ)=NVBPL+LASTV+MOD(J-1,NOWV)+1
      LINV(2,NOL+NHORIZ)=NVBPL+LASTV+MOD(J,NOWV)+1
    3 CONTINUE
C IF THE HORIZONTAL LINES DO NOT DEGENERATE ADD THEIR NUMBER TO LINE COUNT.
      IF(NOWV.EQ.NHORIZ) NOL=NOL+NHORIZ
C SETUP FACETS BETWEEN PRECEDING AND PRESENT LEVELS.
      DO 6 J=1,NHORIZ
      NOF=NOF+1
      INDEXF(NOF)=3
      LINF(1,NOF)=NLUIPL+J
      LINF(2,NOF)=NLUIPL+NHORIZ+J
      IF(LASTV.EQ.1) GO TO 4
      IF(NOWV.EQ.1) GO TO 5
C QUADRILATERAL FACET.
      INDEXF(NOF)=4
      LINF(3,NOF)=NLUIPL+NHORIZ+MOD(J,NHORIZ)+1
      LINF(4,NOF)=NLUIPL+2*NHORIZ+J
      GO TO 6
C UPWARD TRIANGULAR FACET.
    4 LINF(3,NOF)=NLUIPL+MOD(J,NHORIZ)+1
      GO TO 6
C DOWNWARD TRIANGULAR FACET.
    5 LINF(3,NOF)=NLUIPL+NHORIZ+MOD(J,NHORIZ)+1
    6 CONTINUE
C RESET NVBPL AND NLUIPL FOR NEXT PASS.
      NVBPL=NVBPL+LASTV
      NLUIPL=NOL-NHORIZ
      IF(NOWV.EQ.1) NLUIPL=NOL
    7 CONTINUE
      RETURN
      END
```

Program 9.9

Example 9.5

Draw the 'solid' body of figure 9.6. The viewpoint is (15, 20, 25) for figure 9.6a and (2, −35, 5) for figure 9.6b; in both cases, PPD = 33.

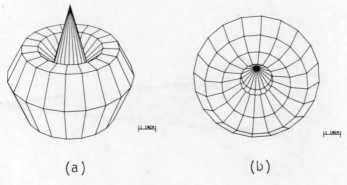

(a)   (b)

Figure 9.6

These are two views of the same object; note that, despite the name, the object is not solid — it is only a thin opaque surface layer. The second figure, figure 9.6b, shows the view of the underside, where we can see inside the body to the undersurface of the cone that forms the top of the object. This is because the first vertical sequence, created in program 9.10, only touches the central axis at one point, the vertex of the upper cone, and so from underneath we can see up 'inside' the object. It is drawn by the Main Program 9.2 calling the following SETUP subroutine.

```
      SUBROUTINE SETUP (Q)
C SETUP AN ELEMENTARY EXAMPLE OF A SOLID BODY OF ROTATION.
      DIMENSION Q(4,4),XLIN(50),YLIN(50)
      COMMON/VERTS/NOV,X(300),Y(300),Z(300),XP(300),YP(300)
      COMMON/LINES/NOL,LINV(2,400)
      COMMON/FACETS/NOF,INDEXF(200),LINF(6,200)
C DATA FOR THE FIRST VERTICAL SEQUENCE.
      DATA XLIN/0.0,1.0,2.0,3.0,4.0,3.0,2.0,1.0/
      DATA YLIN/5.0,1.0,2.0,2.0,0.0,-3.0,-3.0,-1.0/
      NOV=0
      NOL=0
      NOF=0
C ACTUAL SPACE IS IDENTIFIED WITH SETUP SPACE, HENCE THE SETUP TO
C OBSERVER MATRIX R IS EQUAL TO Q.
      CALL ROTSOL (7,20,Q,XLIN,YLIN)
      RETURN
      END
```

Program 9.10

Exercise 9.6
Draw the 'space rocket' of figure 9.7.

In this figure, a hybrid, the 'body of rotation' method is used in conjunction with a subroutine that creates the 'fins' of the rocket.

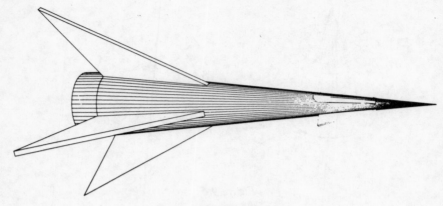

Figure 9.7

EXTENSIONS TO PROGRAMS

It is becoming increasingly obvious that the storage space for our figures is
quickly filled when using these methods; the storage 'housekeeping' is in turn
quite time-consuming. We can increase the size of the COMMON store, but
even this is limited, and it makes the time problem more acute.

   The vertex—line—facet description of objects contains redundant information
— we need only define facets in terms of vertices, and then calculate (rather than
store) the lines from the facet information when they are required. This object
description, though perhaps more efficient, was rejected for this book in the
interest of continuity between 'wire figures' and the Hidden Line Algorithm,
and also for clarity of description. For the same reasons, other more efficient
Hidden Line Algorithms using involved programming techniques (such as
recursive routines using stacks, tree structures, linked lists, etc.) were overlooked
in favour of the more straightforward approach.

   In order to draw involved scenes it is necessary to use these other methods in
complicated variations on the ideas given in this book. The over-all view of space
needs to be divided into sections and the information on these sections efficiently
placed in 'backing store', so that individual sections can be quickly recalled from
store to be dealt with in the usual way. Since these ideas are outside the scope of
this book, this is the obvious point to end our introductory discussion of three-
dimensional graphics.

   Readers who have successfully reached this stage should be ready to tackle
and program the highly sophisticated algorithms necessary to deal with these
complicated diagrams.

10 Computer Movies

The basic idea behind making computer movies is quite straightforward. Using the methods developed in previous chapters, the programmer produces sequences of 16 mm film; each frame from a sequence will differ slightly from the preceding and succeeding frames. The sequences can then be spliced together as is usual with movie films. When a film is projected, normally at 24 frames per second, the scenes on successive frames merge to give the effect of movement in a computer-produced 'cartoon'.

Each frame of the film is assumed to have a drawing area of 11.84 by 9.0 screen inches — these dimensions vary between packages, so check as usual. With the 16 mm film the shorter sides of the frame rectangle are parallel with the two lines of sprocket holes (our usual x-direction), and so it is necessary to rotate the frame through 90° before printing it on the film. Again the ways of achieving this will depend on the implementation of the graphics package; we give a typical example. The routines used are the PLOT subroutine already described in chapter 1, and four others: STARTF, FINISHF, CALCMP and NEWPAGE.

CALL STARTF(3.0, 31.25)

replaces the call to START; the 3.0 parameter specifies the use of 16 mm film, and the 31.25 is a scaling factor that defines the frame size to be 11.84 by 9.0 'inches'.

CALL FINISHF

replaces the call to ENPLOT. The general call to CALCMP is of the form

CALL CALCMP(P1, P2, N, INDEX)

where INDEX specifies one of maybe 20 or more uses of the routine; we only consider three.

(a)   CALL CALCMP(XDUM, YDUM, 1, 9)

Here XDUM and YDUM are irrelevant dummy arguments (usually set to 99); the last two parameters represent a rotation (the parameter 9) through 90° (the parameter 1).

(b)   CALL CALCMP(11.84, 9.0, IDUM, 13)

IDUM is another dummy argument, and the call centres the frame (the entry 13) within a rectangle 11.84 by 9.0 formed by the centres of the sprocket holes. Note that, although the frame is 'centred', the origin is the bottom left-hand corner' of the frame until it is changed by a call to PLOT.

(c)   CALL CALCMP(0, IREP, IDUM, 14)

repeats the previously drawn frame (specified by the 0 entry) IREP times, inclusive of the first time the frame was drawn.

CALL NEWPAGE

is the frame advance facility, without which it is impossible to produce a sequence of frames. In each new frame the scale, rotation and centring is maintained, unless they are changed by further calls to CALCMP; however, the origin, wherever it was in the last frame, is returned to the bottom left-hand corner of the new frame.

Before making the first complete print of a movie (perhaps one of the later examples) it is essential that readers compare these routines against their own implementations by running (say) 10 trial frames. Also, before a production run of any size, it is sensible to check the contents of the film on a 'scope. To do this you may have to write dummy routines for CALCMP, etc. In the interest of efficiency and expenditure (!) it is best to draw every 20th frame, and thence correct any errors before a wasteful and expensive production of film.

The effect of movement may naturally be achieved by painstakingly calculating the scenes in consecutive frames, and laboriously typing in the data for each frame; this is not recommended! We resort to a few simple but nonetheless useful 'tricks of the trade'. We consider five from two-dimensional space (rotation of planar objects, transforming between planar objects, movement of a reference point and/or change of size, 'growing' and variable clipping and/or covering) and discuss two methods in three-dimensional space (movement of the observer, and rotation about an axis), in order to introduce the flavour of movie making.

All these methods have the same central theme. The program will contain a large outer loop; each pass through this loop draws a new frame, and also makes small changes in the parameters required for drawing the frame, thus producing small subtle changes between consecutive frames.

ROTATION OF PLANAR OBJECTS

A planar object is defined by K vertices $\{(X(I), Y(I)) \mid I = 1, \ldots, K\}$, which defines K − 1 lines. The Jth line joins (X(J), Y(J)) to (X(J + 1), Y(J + 1)), and the object is 'closed' if $(X(1), Y(1)) = (X(K), Y(K))$. The object may be drawn by joining these points in order, using the general subroutine JOINUP, which can join up to 100 vertices in this way.

```
      SUBROUTINE JOINUP (K,X,Y)
C ROUTINE TO JOIN CONSECUTIVE POINTS (X(I),Y(I)), I=1,...,K
C THE MAXIMUM VALUE OF K = 100.
      DIMENSION X(100),Y(100)
      CALL PLOT(X(1),Y(1),3)
      DO 1 I=2,K
      CALL PLOT(X(I),Y(I),2)
    1 CONTINUE
      RETURN
      END
```

Program 10.1

An object defined in this way can be rotated in three-dimensional space about an arbitrary axis to produce a new array of K elements (a new object), which can be drawn using the same JOINUP routine. If the rotation is made by small amounts — the same fixed angle per change of frame — then the effect of rotating in three-dimensional space is obtained.

Example 10.1
Draw the block letters 'I', 'A' and 'N' in a movie film of at least M frames (the value of M is input). The 'I' is to rotate about an axis through its centre parallel to the z-direction (into the screen) with a period M/3 frames. The outside of the 'A' is to rotate about the x-direction through its centre (horizontal) with period M/2 frames; the inside of the 'A' stays fixed. Finally 'N' rotates about an axis parallel to the y-axis (vertical) through its centre with period M.

This is where we observe the thorny problem of 'telegraph poles and gaps'; that is, are the objects that we are counting the telegraph poles or the gaps between them? If there are N poles (not in a closed circle) then there are N − 1

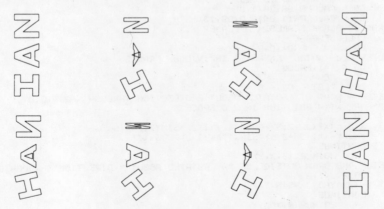

Figure 10.1

gaps. A rotation of period M means that after M changes of frame (that is, gaps) the scene on the film returns to its original form — the frames are the telegraph poles, whence M + 1 frames. Thus the 'I' is in its original form in frames 1, M/3 + 1, 2M/3 and 1 and M + 1, and the 'A' in frames 1, M/2 + 1 and M + 1.

Figure 10.1 shows eight (non-consecutive) frames from the film, that is, (I − 1) M/7 where I = 1, 2, . . . , 8. This method will prove useful for drawing unusual lettering in the advertisements of project 12, chapter 11.

The planar objects 'I', outside of 'A', inside of 'A' and 'N' are stored as vertices in the arrays (XI, YI), (XAO, YAO), (XAI, YAI) and (XN, YN), respectively. Within the outer loop, the objects stored in these arrays are rotated through angles THETA, PHI, (no rotation) and PSI respectively, these angles are incremented by $2\pi \times 3/M$, $2\pi \times 2/M$, zero and $2\pi/M$ radians with each pass.

```
C PROGRAM TO DEMONSTRATE THE ROTATION OF PLANAR OBJECTS.
      DIMENSION XI(13),YI(13),XAO(9),YAO(9),XAI(4),YAI(4),XN(11),YN(11)
      DIMENSION X(13),Y(13)
C SETUP ARRAYS FOR CHARACTERS "I","A" AND "N".
      DATA XI/2*-1.6,2*-2.25,2*-1.6,2*-3.4,2*-2.75,2*-3.4,-1.6/
      DATA YI/1.0,2*0.5,2*-0.5,2*-1.0,2*-0.5,2*0.5,2*1.0/
      DATA XAO/0.25,1.0,0.5,0.375,-0.375,-0.5,-1.0,-0.25,0.25/
      DATA YAO/1.0,2*-1.0,2*-0.6666666,2*-1.0,2*1.0/
      DATA XAI/0.0,0.25,-0.25,0.0/
      DATA YAI/0.333333,-0.333333,-0.333333,0.333333/
      DATA XN/1.5,2.0,2*3.0,2*3.5,3.0,2*2.0,2*1.5/
      DATA YN/2*1.0,-0.3,2*1.0,2*-1.0,0.3,2*-1.0,1.0/
      PI=3.1415926535
C READ IN M, THE TOTAL PERIOD OF ROTATION.
      READ(5,*) M
      MPLUS1=M+1
      OVERM=1.0/FLOAT(M)
C CALCULATE THE INCREMENTS AND INITIAL VALUES OF THE ROTATION ANGLES.
      TI=0.0
      TIB=PI*6*OVERM
      TA=PI*0.5
      TAB=PI*4*OVERM
      TN=0.0
      TNB=PI*2*OVERM
      CALL STARTF(3.0,31.25)
      CALL CALCMP(99,99,1,9)
      CALL CALCMP(11.84,9.0,99,13)
C DRAW 10 BLANK FRAMES ( A LEADER ).
      CALL NEWPAGE
      CALL CALCMP(0,10,99,14)
C OUTER LOOP WHICH GENERATES INDIVIDUAL FRAMES.
      DO 4 I=1,MPLUS1
      CALL NEWPAGE
      CALL PLOT(5.92,4.5,-3)
C SETUP + DRAW "I" ROTATED ABOUT Z DIRECTION THROUGH (-2.5,0.0).
C COMPARE WITH ROTATION IN 2-D SPACE.
      DO 1 J=1,13
      X(J)=(XI(J)+2.5)*COS(TI)+YI(J)*SIN(TI)-2.5
      Y(J)=-(XI(J)+2.5)*SIN(TI)+YI(J)*COS(TI)
    1 CONTINUE
      CALL JOINUP(13,X,Y)
C SETUP AND DRAW OUTSIDE OF "A" ROTATED ABOUT X DIRECTION THROUGH ORIGIN
      DO 2 J=1,9
      Y(J)=YAO(J)*SIN(TA)
    2 CONTINUE
      CALL JOINUP(9,XAO,Y)
C  DRAW INSIDE OF "A" , NO ROTATION.
      CALL JOINUP(4,XAI,YAI)
```

```
C SETUP + DRAW "N" ROTATED ABOUT Y DIRECTION THROUGH (2.5,0.0).
      DO 3 J=1,11
      X(J)=(XN(J)-2.5)*COS(TN)+2.5
   3 CONTINUE
      CALL JOINUP(11,X,YN)
C CHANGE ANGLE OF ROTATION VALUES FOR "I" "A" "N".
      TI=TI+TIB
      TA=TA+TAB
      TN=TN+TNB
   4 CONTINUE
C REPEAT THE LAST FRAME 24 TIMES ( A TRAILER ).
      CALL CALCMP(0,24,99,14)
      CALL FINISHF
      STOP
      END
```

Program 10.2

Exercise 10.1

It is said that the human race is divided into three categories: those who don't watch movies; those who wonder why, in Westerns, the stagecoach wheels seem to rotate the wrong way; and the rest who simply haven't noticed. Write a program that draws the side view of a stagecoach (that is, two wheels are visible), and then simulates the movement of the wheels.

Figure 10.2 shows two consecutive frames, each showing an idealised wheel with six spokes. Figure 10.2b is figure 10.2a rotated anticlockwise about the axle by $45°$ — or is it $60° + 45°$, $120° + 45°$ or even $180° + 45°$, etc.? Or perhaps the rotation is clockwise through $60° - 45° = 15°$, or even clockwise through $60° + 15°$, or $120° + 15°$, etc.? It is this uncertainty that is the reason for the stagecoach wheels moving the wrong way. The brain must make one choice from all the possible angles; if it happens to be the wrong one, then our perception is at odds with reality. The usual subconscious choice is the smallest angle, clockwise or anticlockwise. So in our example, although we intend the wheels to turn through $45°$ anticlockwise, we perceive a rotation of $15°$ clockwise (the wrong way). Naturally if we intend a rotation of $60°$ between consecutive frames then the wheel will appear to stand still. A rotation of $30°$ will cause the wheel to flicker between two positions, and so on. In the problem, let the wheel rotate through an angle θ, anticlockwise, the coach is moving from right to left! The value of θ may be varied (accelerate or decelerate) in order to experiment with the problem of mistaken perception.

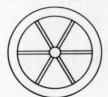 

Figure 10.2

TRANSFORMATION BETWEEN PLANAR OBJECTS

Two planar objects are defined by the two sets of vertices $\{(X1(K), Y1(K)) \mid K = 1, \ldots, N\}$ and $\{(X2(K), Y2(K)) \mid K = 1, \ldots, N\}$. The first figure is drawn in frame 1, and the second in frame M + 1; the intermediate M frame changes cause the objects gradually to transform from one into the other. We look at one simple way of describing these intermediate figures — a method which, although elementary, greatly impresses the uninitiated. We assume that corresponding pairs of defining vertices transform from one to the other along a straight line — the Kth vertex of object 1 into the Kth vertex of object 2 ($K = 1, \ldots, N$). After the Ith change of frame, the vertices will have travelled I/Mth of their allotted line. Again note that there are M changes, so M + 1 frames. Thus the intermediate figure is defined by $\{(X(K), Y(K)) \mid K = 1, \ldots, N\}$ where in the Ith frame

$$(X(K), Y(K)) = (1 - \mu)(X1(K), Y1(K)) + \mu(X2(K), Y2(K)) \text{ and } \mu = (I - 1)/M$$

In each frame the object is drawn by linking the defining vertices with the JOINUP routine of program 10.1.

Example 10.2
Transform between a square and a star in 101 frames.

Since the star has eight points (it will be stored as nine vertices — vertex 1 is the same as vertex 9, and so the figure is closed) the square must also be considered to have eight vertices; we take the corners and midpoints of the sides. Note that the orientation of the vertices in both figures need not be the same, in program 10.3 the square is defined clockwise and the star anticlockwise. Nor do the corresponding vertices have to be in the same part of the frame, however, for simplicity in the example, we take both the square and star centred about the origin. By having different orientations another optical illusion is produced by misleading the brain: as the film progresses the objects as well as transforming between one another, also seem to be rotating in three-dimensional space — a very effective device for project 12.

Figure 10.3 shows frames 1, 11, . . . , 91 and 101 of the film produced by the following program.

```
C PROGRAM TO DEMONSTRATE TRANSFORMATION BETWEEN PLANAR FIGURES.
      DIMENSION X(9),Y(9),X1(9),Y1(9),X2(9),Y2(9)
C (X1,Y1),(X,Y) AND (X2,Y2) ARE ARRAYS DEFINING INITIAL,
C INTERMEDIATE AND FINAL FIGURES.
      DATA X1/0.0,3*3.0,0.0,3*-3.0,0.0/
      DATA Y1/2*3.0,0.0,3*-3.0,0.0,2*3.0/
      DATA X2/3.0,1.0,0.0,-1.0,-3.0,-1.0,0.0,1.0,3.0/
      DATA Y2/0.0,1.0,3.0,1.0,0.0,-1.0,-3.0,-1.0,0.0/
      CALL STARTF (3.0,31.25)
      CALL CALCMP (99,99,1,9)
      CALL CALCMP (11.84,9.0,99,13)
      CALL NEWPAGE
      CALL CALCMP (0,10,99,14)
```

```
C START AT VERTICES IN THE INITIAL FIGURE.
      RMU=0.0
C OUTER LOOP WHICH GENERATES THE FRAMES.
      DO 2 I=1,101
      CALL NEWPAGE
      CALL PLOT(5.92,4.5,-3)
      UMR=1.0-RMU
C CALCULATE INTERMEDIATE FIGURE.
      DO 1 J=1,9
      X(J)=X1(J)*UMR+X2(J)*RMU
      Y(J)=Y1(J)*UMR+Y2(J)*RMU
    1 CONTINUE
      CALL JOINUP(9,X,Y)
C MOVE ALONG THE LINE BETWEEN VERTICES IN INITIAL AND FINAL FIGURES.
      RMU=RMU+0.01
    2 CONTINUE
      CALL CALCMP(0,24,99,14)
      CALL FINISHF
      STOP
      END
```

Program 10.3

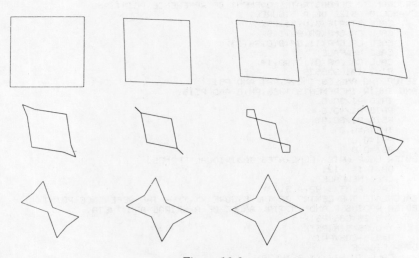

Figure 10.3

Naturally, the more steps used, the smoother the transformation. But beware: it is all too easy for the motion to appear slow and tedious.

MOVEMENT IN SPACE

It is required to move a figure about the screen, and perhaps at the same time to change the size of the figure, and even rotate it. The figure is usually drawn by a subroutine with parameters that specify a reference point for the figure together with information regarding size and rotation. These values can be changed in the outer loop of a movie program to produce the required effect.

Example 10.3

Produce a 'hypnotising' movie, using the subroutine TWIST of exercise 1.4 (figure 1.5). The centre of the figure moves on a circle of radius 0.25 inches and completes its path every 120 frames. The radius of the circle containing the spirals varies between 3.5 and 1.5 inches in a simple harmonic motion of period 80 frames. The spirals also rotate completely once every 60 frames.

Suppose that in the Ith frame, the containing circle has radius R, one of the spirals has initial angle θ and the centre of the figure is the point (X, Y). Then

$$R = 2.5 + \cos[2\pi(I - 1)/80]$$

$$\theta = 2\pi(I - 1)/60$$

$$X = 0.25 \cos[2\pi(I - 1)/120]$$

$$Y = 0.25 \sin[2\pi(I - 1)/120]$$

```
C PROGRAM TO DEMONSTRATE MOVEMENT OF REFERENCE POINT AND
C CHANGE OF SIZE OF A FIGURE.
      CALL STARTF(3.0,31.25)
      CALL CALCMP(99,99,1,9)
      CALL CALCMP(11.84,9.0,99,13)
      CALL NEWPAGE
      CALL CALCMP(0,10,99,14)
      PI=3.1415926535
C SETUP THE ANGLES THETA,PHI AND PSI
C AND THEIR INCREMENTS THEB,PHIB AND PSIB.
      THEB=PI/30.0
      PHIB=PI/40.0
      PSIB=PI/60.0
      THETA=0.0
      PHI=0.0
      PSI=0.0
C OUTER LOOP WHICH GENERATES INDIVIDUAL FRAMES.
      DO 1 I=1,121
      CALL NEWPAGE
      CALL PLOT(5.92,4.5,-3)
C CALCULATE THE CENTRE OF THE FIGURE (X,Y) - THE REFERENCE POINT,
C OUTER RADIUS R AND INITIAL ANGLE OF A SPIRAL ARM THETA.
      X=0.25*COS(PSI)
      Y=0.25*SIN(PSI)
      R=3.0+COS(PHI)
C DRAW FIGURE
      CALL TWIST(X,Y,R,THETA)
C INCREMENT ANGLES.
      THETA=THETA+THEB
      PHI=PHI+PHIB
      PSI=PSI+PSIB
    1 CONTINUE
      CALL CALCMP(0,24,99,14)
      CALL FINISHF
      STOP
      END
```

Program 10.4

GROWING

We start with a blank frame, and as the film progresses extra lines appear until finally a complete figure is drawn. The technique used is to produce a film sequence in which each frame contains exactly the same figure as its predecessor, *plus* a few extra lines. This may be achieved in a number of ways. For example, part of a spiral could be drawn: in the Ith frame of M + 1 frames the spiral rotates through an angle $2n\pi(I - 1)/M$, so that on completion of the alloted M + 1 frames a spiral of n turns is projected.

A more general way is to use the definition of a planar object in terms of N vertices. If there are M + 1 frames between the blank and completed pictures we must discover how much of the diagram is drawn in the Ith frame. We divide the N − 1 lines of the complete picture into subsegments, the total number of subsegments being M. The Kth line, joining vertex K to vertex K + 1, is divided into NOSEG(K) sections, and so

$$NOSEG(1) + NOSEG(2) + \cdots + NOSEG(N - 1) = M$$

For smooth drawing, it is best to make the values of NOSEG proportional to the length of their corresponding lines. Thus, in the Ith frame we draw the first I − 1 subsegments: frame 1 is empty and frame M + 1 contains M subsegments − in other words the N lines are drawn and the figure is complete. There is no need to store the coordinates of the end points of the subsegments; these can be calculated when they are required.

Example 10.4
Grow the stylised tree of figure 10.4 in 151 frames.

Figure 10.4

The tree is divided into two halves; one half is defined by 10 lines (11 vertices) and the other is calculated as the mirror image of the first in the vertical *y*-axis.

```
C PROGRAM TO DEMONSTRATE "GROWING" IN A COMPUTER MOVIE.
      COMMON/TREE/X(11),Y(11),NOSEGS(10)
      CALL STARTF(3.0,31.25)
      CALL CALCMP(99,99,1,9)
      CALL CALCMP(11.84,9.0,99,13)
      CALL NEWPAGE
      CALL CALCMP(0,10,99,14)
C THERE ARE 150 FRAMES IN THE GROWING SEQUENCE.
C EACH TRAVERSAL OF THE LOOP PRODUCES ONE FRAME.
      DO 1 I=1,150
      CALL NEWPAGE
      CALL PLOT(5.92,1.3,-3)
C DRAW THE LEFT HAND AND RIGHT HAND SIDES OF THE PARTIALLY GROWN "TREE".
      CALL DSIDE(1,I)
      CALL DSIDE(-1,I)
    1 CONTINUE
      CALL CALCMP(0,24,99,14)
      CALL FINISHF
      STOP
      END

      SUBROUTINE DSIDE(IS,I)
C ROUTINE TO DRAW PART OF ONE SIDE OF THE "TREE".
C IS=1 FOR RIGHT SIDE , IS=-1 FOR LEFT SIDE.
      COMMON/TREE/X(11),Y(11),NOSEGS(10)
      CALL PLOT(0.0,0.0,3)
      ITAL=I
C DRAW ALL THE LINES GROWN SO FAR , AND PART OF THE GROWING LINE.
      DO 2 J=2,11
      NN=NOSEGS(J-1)
      ITAL=ITAL-NN
      IF(ITAL.GT.0) GO TO 1
C DRAW GROWN PART OF THE LINE WHICH IS GROWING.
      XB=(-ITAL*X(J-1)+X(J)*(NN+ITAL))/NN
      YB=(-ITAL*Y(J-1)+Y(J)*(NN+ITAL))/NN
      CALL PLOT(XB*IS,YB,2)
C IGNORE THE LINES WHICH ARE STILL TO GROW.
      RETURN
C DRAW COMPLETELY THE LINES WHICH ARE FULLY GROWN.
    1 CALL PLOT(X(J)*IS,Y(J),2)
    2 CONTINUE
      RETURN
      END

      BLOCK DATA
C DATA FOR THE IDEALISED "TREE" USED TO DEMONSTRATE GROWING.
      COMMON/TREE/X(11),Y(11),NOSEGS(10)
      DATA X/0.0,2*0.2,3.2,0.2,2.45,0.2,1.7,0.2,0.95,0.0/
      DATA Y/2*0.0,1.0,0.5,2.5,2.0,4.0,3.5,5.5,5.0,6.9/
      DATA NOSEGS/2,8,22,27,18,21,12,18,7,15/
      END
```

Program 10.5

Figure 10.4 shows frames 30, 75, 120 and 151.

VARIABLE CLIPPING AND/OR COVERING

The techniques of chapter 4 are used to clip and/or cover a two-dimensional figure. However, the size of the clipping rectangle (the DX and DY values) is changed by the outer loop of a movie program. If the values of DX and DY are changed in a linear fashion, then the rectangle size appears to accelerate or decelerate — another perception problem that can be used to advantage. Naturally, we do not have to change DX and DY in this way; we could vary the rate of change instead, but the linear change is the most commonly used method.

Example 10.5
A 'tree' of the shape given in example 10.4 is clipped by a rectangle that starts as a point (DX = DY = 0) and changes linearly to a 10 x 8 rectangle, centred on the origin, in the 101st frame. Naturally, the clipping rectangle is drawn on each frame.

The pass of the outer loop with index I(I varies from two to M + 1 = 101; the first (empty) frame is drawn outside the loop) has DX = 5.0(I − 1)/M and DY = 4.0(I − 1)/M.

```
C PROGRAM TO DEMONSTRATE VARIABLE CLIPPING.
      COMMON/OUTER/DX,DY
      COMMON/TREE/X(11),Y(11)
      CALL STARTF(3.0,31.25)
      CALL CALCMP(99,99,1,9)
      CALL CALCMP(11.84,9.0,99,13)
      CALL NEWPAGE
      CALL CALCMP(0,10,99,14)
C THE FIRST RECTANGLE IS NON-EXISTANT SO NOTHING IS DRAWN.
      DX=0.0
      DY=0.0
      DO 1 I=2,101
C INCREMENT THE CLIPPING RECTANGLE VALUES  DX AND DY.
      DX=DX+0.05
      DY=DY+0.04
      CALL NEWPAGE
      CALL PLOT(5.92,4.5,-3)
C DRAW THE RECTANGLE AND THE VISIBLE PARTS OF THE "TREE".
      CALL BOX(DX,DY)
      CALL DSIDE
    1 CONTINUE
      CALL CALCMP(0,24,99,14)
      CALL FINISHF
      STOP
      END

      SUBROUTINE DSIDE
C ROUTINE TO DRAW PART OF TREE VISIBLE THROUGH CLIPPING RECTANGLE.
C NOTE THE "CENTRE" OF THE TREE IS (0.0,3.2) . SO THIS POINT HAS TO
C BE MOVED TO THE CENTRE OF THE CLIPPING RECTANGLE VIZ. SUBTRACT
C 3.2 FROM EACH Y-COORDINATE VALUE.
      COMMON/TREE/X(11),Y(11)
C CLIP THE 10 LINE SEGMENTS ON THE RIGHT AND LEFT OF THE TREE.
      DO 1 I=1,10
      CALL CLIP(X(I),Y(I)-3.2,X(I+1),Y(I+1)-3.2)
      CALL CLIP(-X(I),Y(I)-3.2,-X(I+1),Y(I+1)-3.2)
    1 CONTINUE
      RETURN
      END
```

Program 10.6

BOX is a routine that draws the clipping rectangle, 2DX by 2DY, around the origin. The BLOCK DATA for the tree is the same as in program 10.5. Figure

Figure 10.5

10.5 shows frames 26, 51, 76 and 101 of the movie. We could make the variation of DX and DY non-linear; one simple variation would be to set
DX = 5.0 sin(π(I − 1)/2M) and DY = 4.0 sin(π(I − 1)/2M) in the Ith pass.

Exercise 10.2
Draw the same figure in a movie that varies DX from 5.0 to 3.0 and DY from 1.0 to 4.0. Also make the variation of these values non-linear.

We now demonstrate films of three-dimensional space by returning to the simplified ideas of chapters 6 and 7, so as not to obscure the issues. If films of more complicated spaces are required, for example, using Hidden Line Algorithms, etc., then the following programs should be adjusted accordingly.

MOVEMENT OF THE OBSERVER

So far, we have assumed that the observer is placed at some arbitrary, but fixed, point (EX, EY, EZ) relative to the ACTUAL triad. The ACTUAL system is transformed to the OBSERVER system by the matrix Q, the product of three matrices, $Q = V \times E \times D$, all dependent on EX, EY and EZ (see chapter 6).

If EX, EY and EZ were to change systematically inside the outer loop of a movie program, ACTUAL space remaining fixed, it would have the effect of the observer moving through space while observing some fixed object. Thus the OBSERVE routine of program 6.9 must be slightly altered so that the values of EX, EY and EZ are not read into the routine but instead are input parameters to it.

Example 10.6

A cube is SETUP as in program 6.5; ACTUAL space is identified with SETUP space (that is, matrix $P = I$, the identity matrix). Write a movie program to produce 101 frames in which the observer moves between the points (EX1, EY1, EZ1) and (EX2, EY2, EZ2) — these values are read by the program — and film follows the change in the observer's view along this path.

```
      COMMON/VERTS/NOV,X(300),Y(300),Z(300),XP(300),YP(300)
      COMMON/LINES/NOL,LINV(2,400)
      DIMENSION P(4,4),Q(4,4),R(4,4)
      READ(5,*) PPD
      READ(5,*) EX1,EY1,EZ1,EX2,EY2,EZ2
      CALL STARTF(3.0,31.25)
      CALL CALCMP(99,99,1,9)
      CALL CALCMP(11.84,9.0,99,13)
C FIX THE SETUP COORDINATES OF THE OBJECT AND ALSO
C CALCULATE THE SETUP TO ACTUAL MATRIX P.
      CALL SETUP
      CALL ACTUAL(P)
      RMU=0.0
      DO 3 J=1,101
      CALL NEWPAGE
      CALL PLOT(5.92,4.5,-3)
      UMR=1.0-RMU
C MOVE OBSERVATION POINT (EX,EY,EZ) ALONG THE LINE BETWEEN
C POINTS (EX1,EY1,EZ1) AND (EX2,EY2,EZ2) OF ACTUAL SPACE.
      EX=EX1*UMR+EX2*RMU
      EY=EY1*UMR+EY2*RMU
      EZ=EZ1*UMR+EZ2*RMU
      DIST=SQRT(EX*EX+EY*EY+EZ*EZ)
      CALL OBSERVE(EX,EY,EZ,Q)
      CALL MULT(Q,P,R)
C R IS THE SETUP TO OBSERVER MATRIX FOR EACH NEW OBSERVATION POINT.
C FIND (XX,YY,ZZ) , THE COORDINATES OF THE OBJECT IN THE NEW
C OBSERVATION SPACE.  ALSO CALCULATE (XP(I),YP(I)), I=1,...,NOV,
C THEIR PERSPECTIVE TRANSFORMS.
      DO 1 I=1,NOV
      XX=R(1,1)*X(I)+R(1,2)*Y(I)+R(1,3)*Z(I)+R(1,4)
      YY=R(2,1)*X(I)+R(2,2)*Y(I)+R(2,3)*Z(I)+R(2,4)
      ZZ=R(3,1)*X(I)+R(3,2)*Y(I)+R(3,3)*Z(I)+R(3,4)+DIST
      XP(I)=XX*PPD/ZZ
      YP(I)=YY*PPD/ZZ
    1 CONTINUE
C PLOT THE LINE SEGMENTS IN THE OBJECT.
      DO 2 I=1,NOL
      I1=LINV(1,I)
      I2=LINV(2,I)
      CALL PLOT(XP(I1),YP(I1),3)
      CALL PLOT(XP(I2),YP(I2),2)
    2 CONTINUE
C GET THE NEXT "MU" VALUE.
      RMU=RMU+0.01
    3 CONTINUE
      CALL FINISHF
      STOP
      END
```

Program 10.7

ROTATION OF AN OBJECT ABOUT A GIVEN AXIS

Again in chapter 6 we saw that the SETUP—ACTUAL matrix P of an object rotated by an angle ψ about the line $p + \mu d$ is given by the product of seven matrices, thus

$$P = F^{-1} \times G^{-1} \times H^{-1} \times W \times H \times G \times F$$

where $F, G, H, F^{-1}, G^{-1}, H^{-1}$ relate to moving the axis of rotation on to the positive z-axis, and back again. Matrix W effects the rotation of the object (that is, space) through the angle ψ about the new z-axis created by $H \times G \times F$.

In a movie program that produces one complete rotation of an object, P has to be recalculated inside the outer loop. We assume that the observer stays fixed, and so the OBSERVER matrix Q is created once only — outside the loop. Similarly F, G, H, F^{-1}, G^{-1} and H^{-1} are constant throughout the program, and these also are calculated once only outside the loop; in fact, their values are stored as two product matrices $P1 = Q \times F^{-1} \times G^{-1} \times H^{-1}$ and $P2 = H \times G \times F$ for efficiency.

Suppose that after each frame the object is rotated by a further angle ψ; then we calculate the SETUP—OBSERVER matrix R as follows. In the first frame

$$R = Q \times F^{-1} \times G^{-1} \times H^{-1} \times I \times H \times G \times F$$

$$= P1 \times P2 = Q \quad (R = P1 \times P2; P1 = P1 \times W)$$

After one frame

$$R = P1 \times W \times P2 \quad (R = P1 \times P2; P1 = P1 \times W)$$

After two frames

$$R = P1 \times W^2 \times P2 \quad (R = P1 \times P2; P1 = P1 \times W)$$

Correspondingly, after I frames

$$R = P1 \times W^I \times P2 \quad (R = P1 \times P2; P1 = P1 \times W)$$

The large number of matrix products required as I increases can be greatly simplified by the fixed pair of matrix products shown inside the brackets above. All these ideas are incorporated in the next example.

Example 10.7

Write a movie program that demonstrates the rotation of a cube about the axis $(1, 1, 1) + \mu(1, -1, -1)$. The movie is to complete the rotation after 101 frames.

```
COMMON/VERTS/NOV,X(300),Y(300),Z(300),XP(300),YP(300)
COMMON/LINES/NOL,LINV(2,400)
COMMON DIST,PPD
DIMENSION F(4,4),FM(4,4),G(4,4),GM(4,4),H(4,4),HM(4,4),W(4,4)
DIMENSION P(4,4),Q(4,4),R(4,4),P1(4,4),P2(4,4)
READ(5,*) PPD
C FIX THE SETUP COORDINATES OF THE OBJECT AND CREATE THE
```

```
C ACTUAL TO OBSERVER MATRIX Q.
      CALL SETUP
      CALL OBSERVE (Q)
      CALL STARTF (3.0,31.25)
      CALL CALCMP (99,99,1,9)
      CALL CALCMP (11.84,9.0,99,13)
C CALCULATE MATRICES F,G,H,FM,GM,HM,W.
      CALL TRAN (1.0,1.0,1.0,F)
      CALL TRAN (-1.0,-1.0,-1.0,FM)
      CALL ANGLE (-1.0,1.0,THETA)
      CALL ROT (3,THETA,G)
      CALL ROT (3,-THETA,GM)
      DD=SQRT (2.0)
      CALL ANGLE (DD,-1.0,THETA)
      CALL ROT (2,THETA,H)
      CALL ROT (2,-THETA,HM)
      PSI=3.1415926535*0.02
      CALL ROT (3,-PSI,W)
C P1 = Q * FM * GM * HM     AND     P2 = H * G * F
      CALL MULT (Q,FM,P)
      CALL MULT (GM,HM,R)
      CALL MULT (P,R,P1)
      CALL MULT (H,G,P)
      CALL MULT (P,F,P2)
      DO 5 J=1,101
      CALL NEWPAGE
      CALL PLOT (5.92,4.5,-3)
C THE SETUP TO OBSERVER MATRIX R = P1 * P2
      CALL MULT (P1,P2,R)
C RESET  P1 = P1 * W
      CALL MULT (P1,W,P)
      DO 2 L=1,4
      DO 1 M=1,4
      P1 (L,M) =P (L,M)
    1 CONTINUE
    2 CONTINUE
C FIND (XX,YY,ZZ) , THE COORDINATES OF THE OBJECT IN THE NEW
C OBSERVATION SPACE.  ALSO CALCULATE (XP(I),YP(I)), I=1,...,NOV,
C THEIR PERSPECTIVE TRANSFORMS.
      DO 3 I=1,NOV
      XX=R (1,1) *X (I) +R (1,2) *Y (I) +R (1,3) *Z (I) +R (1,4)
      YY=R (2,1) *X (I) +R (2,2) *Y (I) +R (2,3) *Z (I) +R (2,4)
      ZZ=R (3,1) *X (I) +R (3,2) *Y (I) +R (3,3) *Z (I) +R (3,4) +DIST
      XP (I) =XX*PPD/ZZ
      YP (I) =YY*PPD/ZZ
    3 CONTINUE
C PLOT THE LINE SEGMENTS IN THE OBJECT.
      DO 4 I=1,NOL
      I1=LINV (1,I)
      I2=LINV (2,I)
      CALL PLOT (XP (I1) ,YP (I1) ,3)
      CALL PLOT (XP (I2) ,YP (I2) ,2)
    4 CONTINUE
    5 CONTINUE
      CALL FINISHF
      STOP
      END
```

Program 10.8

This program uses the SETUP of program 6.5, and the OBSERVE routine of program 6.9. No ACTUAL routine is explicitly given; the implicit SETUP–ACTUAL matrix *P* is calculated in the movie loop.

These are just a few ideas (there are many many more) for using the medium of movie film, which are presented in order to give a taste of its potential. The

subject matter of the films has been deliberately kept trivial; it is the ideas behind
the films that are important, and they have wide-ranging applications in
educational films, television presentation and advertisements.

The programs have, to a great extent, been kept in modular form, so that
individual modules (subroutines) can be treated in isolation. We have seen that
this may lead to inefficiency (the reason that we do not use an ACTUAL routine
in program 10.8). So when it comes to producing large production run programs,
be prepared to 'cannibalise' any or all of the programs given in this book! Readers
should also be aware of problems implicit in the production of three-dimensional
films. The combination of large numbers of arithmetic operations (as in the
repeated recalculation of W in example 10.8) may lead to rounding errors
when using computers with limited word length. Know your machine! Also note
that in the hidden line algorithms, the vertex data generated in SETUP routines
is overwritten in the X, Y and Z arrays during the transformation between
SETUP and OBSERVER spaces. If only one picture is drawn this is not a
problem, but in movies, changes in ACTUAL or OBSERVER space necessitate
new transformations of the original SETUP data. Hence the SETUP vertices
must be stored elsewhere for this repeated use.

11 Projects

Up to this point the exercises, although intellectually stretching, have been limited and have not varied greatly from the ideas in the accompanying text. In order to gain confidence in computer graphics it is essential to tackle a number of *major* projects; and if the programs are open ended then so much the better. Although it is hoped that readers will devise their own set of projects, there is also a list of suitable programming tasks, together with hints and explanatory diagrams where necessary.

PROJECT 1

Study the graphics packages available to you. There will be routines for drawing not only SYMBOLs (see chapter 4), but also NUMBERs (decimal digits), AXIS (labelled coordinate axes), etc. (Capital letters are used here because these are three routines available in the Calcomp library.)

Use these subroutines to create data graphs similar to figure 11.1, which was produced by one of my students. Any data base will do for practice! Write your

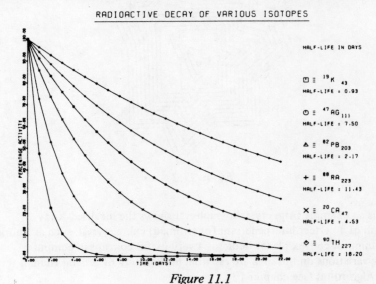

Figure 11.1

own routines to produce coordinate axes for use with discrete data — the packages never give you exactly what is required. Devise a package that draws pie charts, histograms and other forms of pictorial data description.

PROJECT 2

Suppose we are given two coplanar convex bodies, each containing a common point c, and defined by the sequence of vector points $\{p_1, p_2, \ldots, p_n = p_1\}$ and $\{q_1, q_2, \ldots, q_m = q_1\}$. Find the new body, not necessarily convex, containing c and defined by the vectors $\{r_1, r_2, \ldots, r_k = r_1\}$, which is the union of the two bodies, that is, the smallest figure to contain all the lines and points of the first two figures. *Hint*: use the 'inside' and 'outside' techniques of example 2.6.

Figure 11.2 shows a slice through an 'interpenetrant cubic onion', that is, an object that is composed of a series of concentric surfaces (or 'skins'), each skin being similar to figure 8.2. The complete slice is the combination of slices through individual surfaces; each single slice is the union of the slices through the two cubes that form the skin. Thus the above technique can be used. Note that the slice may be such that the two convex bodies (that is, the slices through the two cubes of each skin) do not intersect; furthermore, the slicing plane may miss one or both of the cubes.

Figure 11.2

This is an example from crystallography; it shows the idealised X-ray topograph of a perfect interpenetrant (or twinned) cubic crystal, such as fluorite.

The union of convex planar bodies is a very useful concept in computer graphics; variations on this idea are essential in the study of general Hidden Surface Algorithms (see chapter 12).

PROJECT 3

Draw the outline of the ground-floor plan of a house, adding windows, doors which may rotate on hinges, interior walls, etc. Then produce subroutines that draw diagrammatic representations of tables, chairs, a television set and all forms of household furniture, viewed from above. Use the D–D–D (draw–drag–delete) method of chapter 4 to move the furniture about the house. The program should give information about whether the articles 'overlap', and it must also create a measure for the utilisation of space and thus find the 'best position' for the furniture.

PROJECT 4

Write an interactive program that enables the user to draw diagrams composed of straight lines and curves (for example, quarter and semicircular arcs) on the graphics console using the cursor and grid methods described in Chapter 4.
   A straight line is drawn by a subroutine which recognises the cursor-specified end points of the line. Similarly, the circular arcs are drawn by a routine that is given the centre and start point of the arc, specified by the cursor, whence the radius can be calculated. The angular size of the arc can be read from the keyboard, or it too can be obtained from cursor values.
   Then use the program to design patterns for wallpapers and fabrics.

PROJECT 5

Produce general pattern-making programs. In recent years computer-drawn patterns have proved very popular for illustrating books, pamphlets and advertising literature.
   For example, the movie program (program 10.8) for rotating a cube about a given axis can be used to draw diagrams like figure 11.3: simply take the calls to NEWPAGE out of the code. By changing the axis of rotation, observation point, etc., a whole series of similar pictures can be developed. We could smooth out the jagged edges surrounding the figure by joining the corresponding vertices of the cube as it is rotated, and there are many other variations on this theme that can be used to make new series of shapes.
   Another method would be to set the vertices of a triangle to be points on three different Spirographs (program 1.7). If N is the lowest common multiple (l.c.m.) of the three path sizes, then a balanced diagram can be drawn by joining N successive points on the paths − perhaps joining the corresponding vertices of each triangle as they are calculated.
   The latter two ideas are simple variations on the 'pin-and-cotton' diagrams of chapter 1; however, far more involved and sophisticated patterns may be drawn.

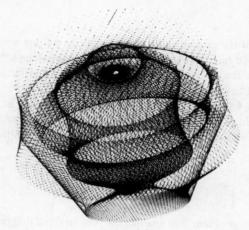

Figure 11.3

Figure 11.4 shows the orthographic projection of the solid body that is common to 24 equiradial cyclinders whose axes meet at the origin. All the facets have elliptical edges and, unlike the planar objects seen so far, these are sections cut from the surface of a cylinder. This is another example taken from crystallography — a treasure trove of patterns! It is the idealised form of a crystal with cubic symmetry that has partially dissolved.

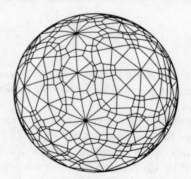

Figure 11.4

PROJECT 6

Use the techniques of chapter 9 to produce skeleton pictures of technical equipment, for example, parts of car engines — pistons, camshafts, etc. — in orthographic or perspective views. Figure 11.5 shows a skeleton picture of an aerosol cap, incorporating the washer, spring and casing of figure 9.5. The individual items may be drawn on different parts of the screen, exploding the figure; thus the interference caused by overdrawing can be eliminated.

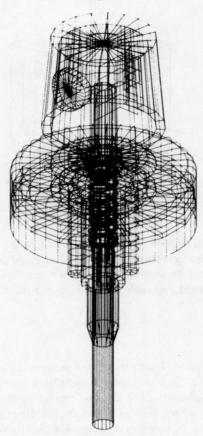

Figure 11.5

PROJECT 7

Use the green and red pens of a paper plotter to produce stereoscopic views of 'ball and spoke' chemical molecular models.

PROJECT 8

Experiment with optical illusions and 'impossible figures'; we have already seen some movie examples in chapter 10. Get ideas from the many books on the subject and produce diagrams like figure 11.6.

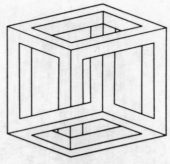

Figure 11.6

PROJECT 9

Spiders use algorithms to fashion their webs! Simulate the construction of the orb web of the common garden spider, in an educational movie demonstrating web building. Also include an idealised spider moving about the web. It can be simply a circle with eight moveable jointed legs, or a much more sophisticated hairy beast.

PROJECT 10

Construct a wide range of Moiré patterns (sometimes these are called net-curtain patterns) on microfilm. Such patterns are made by drawing a large number of lines (and curves); the variety of small areas created by the intersections are perceived as a cloudy effect, such as that in the middle of figure 11.7, which is formed by four sets of 80 concentric circles. The density of lines must be carefully chosen: if there are too many lines then the Moiré pattern is blurred through overexposure; if there are too few, the pattern is not discernible.

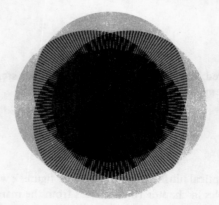

Figure 11.7

Then use the clipping routines of chapter 4 to isolate areas of the pattern with the most outstanding Moiré effect; for example, delete the outer sections of figure 11.7 where there are relatively few intersections.

PROJECT 11

Produce an interactive crossword puzzle maker. The program should draw a variable M by N crossword grid; some of these squares are 'blacked out' after indicating them with a pen sensor or cursor. Clues must be numbered and written below and alongside the puzzle. The solutions to the puzzle, and the numbers of special squares, must be added to the diagram by a combination of keyboard and pen sensor. Black squares, clues, solutions and numbers must be capable of deletion whenever the compiler of the crossword changes his mind about a clue during the creation of the puzzle.

PROJECT 12

Write programs to produce 20- or 30-second advertisement movie films; any product will do for the subject of the film. All the methods described in chapter 10 may be used, as well as bodies of rotation, Hidden Line Algorithms, etc. Figure 11.8 shows one frame of a Land Rover® advertisement produced by another of my students.

Figure 11.8

PROJECT 13

Construct a variety of mazes (rectangular or circular) on an interactive graphics console. Incorporate into it a facility that enables users to try and find their way through the maze, using a cursor to plot the path. Also program the 'best path' through each maze.

PROJECT 14

Write a program that draws orthographic projections of simple three-dimensional surfaces, similar to that in figure 11.9. The simple surfaces are defined by the 'y-value', which is a single-valued function of x and z. Figure 11.9 shows $y = 3 \sin \sqrt{(x^2 + z^2)}$, that is, $f(x, y, z) \equiv y - 3 \sin \sqrt{(x^2 + z^2)}$.

We may approach the problem by calculating NOX by NOZ points on the surface and assuming that the x-values vary from XBOT to XTOP and the z-values from ZBOT to ZTOP (XBOT < XTOP and ZBOT < ZTOP). The (I, J)th point (x, y, z) on the surface is given by

$$x = \text{XTOP} + (\text{XBOT} - \text{XTOP})(\text{I} - 1)/\text{NOX} - 1)$$

$$z = \text{ZTOP} + (\text{ZBOT} - \text{ZTOP})(\text{J} - 1)/\text{NOZ} - 1)$$

and y is a simple function of these x and z-values.

An x-sequence of lines is one where the NOZ points with the same x-value are joined in order, to form NOZ − 1 line segments. A z-sequence of NOX − 1 line segments is defined in a similar manner.

The whole surface is to be orthographically projected from the observation point (EX, EY, EZ), where both EX and EZ are positive; this may be done in three ways.

(1) Every x-sequence is orthographically projected together with the z = ZTOP and z = ZBOT sequences. Naturally some of these lines may be hidden from view, and so it is necessary to develop a special Hidden Line Algorithm; we could use the general Algorithm, but this would require enormous store and time usage! The x = XTOP and z = ZTOP sequences are joined to form the Upper Visible Boundary (UVB); they simultaneously form the Lower Visible Boundary (LVB). By passing through the remaining NOX − 1 x-sequences, from x = XTOP − (XTOP − XBOT)/(NOX − 1) to x = XBOT, in order, we draw the surface thus. With each new x-sequence, some parts will be below the UVB and some above. If they are above then they are visible and so are drawn; these visible parts are then used to alter the UVB. Similarly if part of an x-sequence is below the LVB, it is drawn and the LVB altered. Note that the lines of a new sequence need not cross the UVB or LVB at one of the NOX × NOZ surface projected points; this must be allowed for in the calculation of the new UVBs and LVBs. Figure 11.9a was drawn in this way.

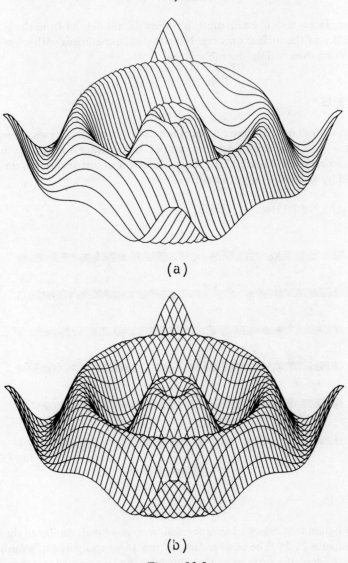

(a)

(b)

Figure 11.9

(2) Repeat the above process, with the same initial UVB and LVB, but instead move through the *z*-sequences.

(3) The third way is to superimpose methods (1) and (2), which results in a picture similar to figure 11.9b. If this method is used, then some anomalous triangular facets will appear; these are parts of the surface that are visible on only one of the two superimposed pictures. Strictly speaking

these facets should be invisible, but they do not detract from the visual quality of the surface drawing. Nevertheless, experiment with ways of deleting these visible—invisible facets.

PROJECT 15

Construct a program that draws musical notation — bar lines, staves, quavers, rests, etc. — on a graphics screen or microfilm. Incorporate it in another program that composes music. Figure 11.10 shows the result of one such program developed by another of my students.

Figure 11.10

PROJECT 16

Write a program that draws a hemispherical 'wooden' bowl, similar to the one shown in figure 11.11. The bowl is carved from a tree composed of a number of co-axial cylinders; the surfaces of the cylinders (the tree rings) form the patterns on the base of the bowl; that is, they are the curves of intersection of the hemisphere with the cylinders. The parameters that uniquely define one bowl are the equitorial plane of the bowl, the radii of the bowl and cylinders and the position of the centre of the bowl relative to the axis of the cylinders. *Hint*: imagine that the axis of the cylinders is the x-axis, and that the y–z plane ($x = 0$) is one of the cross-sections through the cylinders, and the centre of the bowl is on the y-axis. Then vary the most suitable of the coordinates (x, say) between its calculable limits, find the y-values (we can ignore the z by taking an

Figure 11.11

orthographic projection) and join them in sequence. But be careful: for any
value of x, there may be more than one value of y.

PROJECT 17

The coordinate values used in this book are system dependent, that is,
dependent on the screen inch and initial position of the origin. All commercial
software define such systems but they will differ from one another. There are
many three-dimensional graphics applications where we wish to use programs
which are independent of such systems. In the real world objects are measured
in miles or millimetres, etc., so it is sensible to store coordinates in such units.
Hence it is necessary to scale a picture from the real to screen coordinates. To
do this the program must first be given the size of the screen and position of
the origin.

For an orthographic picture the program should calculate the coordinates of
every vertex (in the real units of OBSERVER space), and scale them so they
just fit on the screen. There is no need to multiply the x- and y-coordinates of
every vertex by the scaling factor SC (say), because most packages have a
subroutine similar to

CALL FACTOR(SC)

which automatically scales the PLOT, SYMBOL, etc., calls about the origin by
the amount SC. Naturally if a series of orthographic plots is planned, SC
should be kept fixed for all the diagrams.

As for perspective views, the machine is given PRAT, the ratio of the
distance of the eye from the screen, to the half depth of the screen (usually 4).
Then the value of PPD is set to PRAT and the point (XI, YI, ZI) is transformed
to (XI*PRAT/(ZI+DIST), YI*PRAT/(ZI+DIST)) whose values are dimensionless;
both must be less than unity in absolute value for (XI, YI, ZI) to be in the
pyramid of vision. The origin is centred on the screen and SC set to the half
screen depth (in screen inches) to get a system-independent perspective picture.
Try these ideas on the given programs.

12 Conclusion: What Next?

Although this book is only an introduction to computer graphics, we have nevertheless studied some sophisticated programs and ideas. These programs should be studied thoroughly and completely understood, and perhaps reorganised to make them more efficient in particular special cases. The methods implemented in them are more than adequate for the majority of graphics problems; any complexity will be implicit in the underlying mathematics of the problem, rather than in the graphics. It is evidently impossible to separate computer graphics from coordinate geometry; a complete understanding of two and three-dimensional objects in the theories of euclidean and cartesian coordinate geometry and trigonometry is essential. Similarly, a good knowledge of efficient programming techniques (of coding and storage manipulation) is necessary in order to cope with the drawing of large complicated scenes. In fact, Fortran may not be the best language for some involved pictorial problems; languages with the facility of implicit data structures, such as Pascal or Algol 68, may be more suitable for computer graphics at the research level. However, for most commercial and scientific uses, Fortran is the most widely used and suitable programming language; that is why it was chosen for this book. Even so, the algorithms have been written in such a way that they can be easily translated into these other languages with a minimum of effort. Also most structures, such as linear lists and trees, and the use of a 'garbage collector', can be implemented by competent Fortran programmers using arrays with the SHIFT and .AND. operators. Even recursive calls can be incorporated into Fortran programs by writing small linking subprograms in machine code.

What next? There is one obvious answer — colour graphics. We have concentrated on line drawing thus far; there has been no means of filling in areas other than by shading with lines. Raster scan devices, similar to 625 line television sets, have the capacity to colour in areas of the screen. There is, however, a loss of accuracy in line definition; when a line runs almost parallel to a 'scan line' it will appear very jagged. The screen is a matrix of coloured dots (pixels), and this means that the resolution of lines is not as good as in 'storage tubes', 'refresh devices' and microfilm.

Colours are usually specified by an integer code that can be redefined from the keyboard, before or after the picture is drawn. Depending on the sophistication (that is, cost!) of the raster 'scope, the colours can be manipulated in a variety of ways: perhaps changing the mix of the red—blue—green combination that is the basis of all colour television pictures; or combining groups of coloured dots into patterns, and filling areas with these patterns; or other much more involved manipulations.

Because the screen is a matrix of discrete points (the coloured dots), the picture-generating code of the processor for the device will refer to a point on the screen by its absolute position in the dot matrix — usually relative to the bottom left-hand corner (b.l.c.) dot, which has coordinates (0, 0), that is, by the pair of integers (i, j), where the required point is i dots beyond and to the right of the b.l.c. dot, and j dots above it. For example, the Tektronix 4027, a typical middle-range device, has a dot matrix where i varies from 0 to 639 and j from 0 to 405; at any one time there are eight basic colours C0, C1, . . . , C7, which are chosen from a possible 64 colours, and these eight colours may be combined in pairs to form patterns of 8 by 14 dots.

Rather than work with the awkward integer positional values, the available software normally translates the integer pairs into real-number pairs which lie in arbitrarily predefined ranges, by dividing by a fixed scaling factor. Thus, we are left with real x–y-values, the coordinate form we have used throughout this book. In fact, the same process occurs in refresh tubes, and in storage tubes (like the Tektronix 4010) — something we have conveniently ignored until now. The call to START translates from integer screen coordinates into real pairs; the parameter of the routine, 2 in our case, is a code that defines the range of values and a new screen origin.

The translation between integer and real interpretations of the screen leads to another form of the 'telegraph poles and gaps' problem mentioned in chapter 10. Suppose that we scale the picture (by dividing by 40), so that $(0.0, 0.0) \equiv (0, 0)$, and $(1.0, 0.0) \equiv (40, 0)$. How many dots make up a horizontal line of length 1.0: 39, 40 or 41? In other words, does the line contain neither, one or both of the end points (dots)? How many make up a horizontal line of length 2.0: 79, 80 or 81; and for such a line of length 3.0, is it 119, 120 or 121? For consistency, we would expect the answers to be 40, 80 and 120, respectively. However, this is not normally the case; the answer depends on how a line is defined. Usually a line is specified by its end points, and thus includes them, and so 41, 81 and 121 are the usual respective solutions. This leads to an apparent paradox: a horizontal line of length 2.0 is shorter (by one dot) than the combined length of two horizontal lines, both of length 1.0. The problem is further complicated in the case of non-horizontal and non-vertical lines, because of the jaggedness caused when the lines cross the 'scan lines' of the raster screen. This problem can be ignored in line drawings, but it leads to very real difficulties when it comes to colouring in areas (see later).

With these limitations understood, it is possible to implement all the Calcomp library routines, so that the raster screen can be used simply as another line-drawing 'scope — coloured lines, of course! But this would be a dreadful waste of resources. Colouring in areas is no more difficult than drawing lines, after all; the techniques of manipulating two and three-dimensional space are the same whether drawing lines or filling in areas. Naturally there must be further routines for colouring in specified areas; if there are not, it is a simple job to write Fortran subroutines, composed mostly of WRITE and FORMAT statements, that return series of picture-generating code instructions to do the required tasks. Different devices will have different generating codes, but they are all very similar.

Two typical subroutines would be

SUBROUTINE DISC(IC, X, Y, R, ANG1, ANG2)

which draws that part of a disc of radius R, centred at (X, Y), and formed by the radius sweeping between angles ANG1 and ANG2, in a colour with code IC; and

SUBROUTINE POLY(IC, N, X, Y)

probably a more useful routine, which uses colour IC to fill in the facet bounded by the first N points defined by arrays X and Y. Thence, colouring in facets is as simple as drawing lines; just call the above routine with the correct parameters. But remember that if two facets have a common boundary, then their areas overlap in a finite non-zero area, which is the aggregation of the dots that define the line. Thus, the order in which facets are drawn is important. Nevertheless, the real problem still lies in setting up objects in space and projecting their vertices into points on the screen — and this has already been dealt with. There is one major exception to this rather sweeping statement: the console builds up a picture, coloured layer on coloured layer, and hence some areas may be initially filled in with one colour and later covered by another. Thus the order in which facets are coloured is very important, in order to cope with this hidden surface problem.

For most elementary purposes, this order will be specified absolutely by the programmer; however, in more complex pictures such as a colour version of the housing estate of figure 9.3, the relative positions of the facets (that is, the walls and roofs) are unknown until the observer point (EX, EY, EZ) is input. So a Hidden Surface (or Hidden Facet) Algorithm is necessary; some facets will be drawn completely, others will be partially or totally obscured.

The easiest way to achieve this is to 'cheat'! Add an extra facility to the Hidden Line Program, so that figures are subdivided and drawn as a patchwork scene. Then the keyboard can be used to fill in the facets, exactly like a colouring book. But beware: it may happen that facet A is in front of (>) facet B, facet B > facet C and facet C > facet A; so which order do we choose? The answer is none of them: the facets have to be subdivided so that such unordered configurations do not occur.

Such cheating is not satisfactory; a proper Hidden Surface Algorithm is the only sensible solution. Again the data for the scene are stored in the COMMON blocks /VERTS/, /LINES/ and /FACETS/, but now we also need information about the colour of the facets. This can be defined absolutely and stored in /FACETS/ as the array ICOL, which is generated by the SETUP and 'brick' routines, or it can be generated when required. For example, an object may be all one general colour but, depending on the position of a bright light source, the facets will be a variety of shades of this basic colour, a shade being a function of the angle at which the light strikes the facet.

As with Hidden Line Algorithms, there are many types of Hidden Surface Algorithm — both special-purpose and general. For example, it is easy to change program 8.3, the special Hidden Line Algorithm for a convex body containing the origin, into a Hidden Surface Algorithm for use with the same type of object (program 12.1).

```
      SUBROUTINE HIDSURF
C SIMPLE HIDDEN SURFACE ALGORITHM FOR USE WITH CONVEX BODIES
C CONTAINING THE ORIGIN.
      DIMENSION IND(6),XC(6),YC(6)
      COMMON/VERTS/NOV,X(300),Y(300),Z(300),XP(300),YP(300)
      COMMON/LINES/NOL,LINV(2,400)
      COMMON/FACETS/NOF,INDEXF(200),LINF(6,200),ICOL(200)
      COMMON DIST,PPD
C CHECK EACH FACET.
      DO 3 I=1,NOF
      I1=LINF(1,I)
      I2=LINF(2,I)
C FROM FIRST TWO LINES IN I'TH FACET FIND IV1,IV2 AND IV3 ,
C THE INDICES OF THREE DIFFERENT POINTS IN THE FACET.
      IV1=LINV(1,I1)
      IV2=LINV(2,I1)
      IV3=LINV(1,I2)
      IF(IV1.EQ.IV3.OR.IV2.EQ.IV3) IV3=LINV(2,I2)
C CALCULATE THE PLANE A.X + B.Y + C.Z = D CONTAINING THESE POINTS.
      DX1=X(IV1)-X(IV2)
      DY1=Y(IV1)-Y(IV2)
      DZ1=Z(IV1)-Z(IV2)
      DX3=X(IV3)-X(IV2)
      DY3=Y(IV3)-Y(IV2)
      DZ3=Z(IV3)-Z(IV2)
      A=DY1*DZ3-DY3*DZ1
      B=DZ1*DX3-DZ3*DX1
      C=DX1*DY3-DX3*DY1
C (X(IV1),Y(IV1),Z(IV1)) LIES IN THIS PLANE THUS ....
      D=A*X(IV1)+B*Y(IV1)+C*Z(IV1)
C (0.0,0.0,0.0) AND (0.0,0.0,-DIST) LIE ON OPPOSITE SIDES OF THE
C FACET IF F IS LESS THAN 0.0 .
      F=1.0+C*DIST/D
      IF(F.GE.0.0) GO TO 3
C THE FACET IS VISIBLE SO COLOUR IT IN.
C ARRAY IND HOLDS THE IXX VERTEX INDICES OF THE VISIBLE FACET.
C IND TAKES ONE INDEX FROM EACH LINE IN THE FACET - THAT VERTEX ON
C BOTH THE PRESENT AND NEXT LINES.
      IND(1)=LINV(1,I1)
      IF(IND(1).NE.LINV(1,I2).AND.IND(1).NE.LINV(2,I2)) IND(1)=LINV(2,I1)
      IXX=INDEXF(I)
      DO 1 J=2,IXX
      JJ=LINF(J,I)
      IND(J)=LINV(1,JJ)
      IF(IND(J).EQ.IND(J-1)) IND(J)=LINV(2,JJ)
    1 CONTINUE
C PLACE THE COORDINATES OF THE VISIBLE FACET IN THE XC AND YC ARRAYS.
      DO 2 J=1,IXX
      XC(J)=XP(IND(J))
      YC(J)=YP(IND(J))
    2 CONTINUE
C COLOUR IN THE POLYGON DEFINED BY THE XC AND YC ARRAYS.
      CALL POLY(ICOL(I),IXX,XC,YC)
    3 CONTINUE
      RETURN
      END
```

Program 12.1

   This subroutine would be called from a Main Program which has one change from program 9.2: the call to HIDDEN is replaced by one to HIDSURF; all other routines stay the same. Inherent in the simple HIDDEN routine is the need to find whether a facet is visible or not; hence the Hidden Surface Algorithm for this simple case is not as complicated as the Hidden Line Algorithm. This is not generally true! When the reader can produce such a general subroutine, then he or she can claim to be a 'computer graphics expert'. It goes without saying that an efficient general Hidden Surface Algorithm is a valuable commercial asset. The main purpose of this book is to lead the reader to this final major project. All the programming tools have been given: space manipulation, object definition, 'inside and outside' of planar convex bodies, etc. It is up to the reader to combine all the pieces into the final program. Good luck!

   The study of computer graphics is still at an early stage in its development. In the next-few years there will be many new discoveries and unusual applications of the subject, all generated by the steady decrease in the price of graphics devices. The drop in costs is leading to a rapid growth of commerical applications: a picture is far more acceptable than a massive table of numbers. New design fields are opening up; technological and architectural design, pictorial representation of large numerical data bases, visual simulation models, television advertising – the list goes on and on. Soon the computer graphics console and accompanying hard copy devices will be as common a tool as the visual display unit is today. The future of computer graphics looks very bright indeed.

Index